ASHE Higher Education Report: Volume 31, Number 5
Kelly Ward, Lisa E. Wolf-Wendel, Series Editors

From Main Street to Wall Street

The Transformation of For-Profit
Higher Education

Kevin Kinser

From Main Street to Wall Street: The Transformation of For-Profit Higher Education
Kevin Kinser
ASHE Higher Education Report: Volume 31, Number 5
Kelly Ward, Lisa Wolf-Wendel, Series Editors

ISSN 1551-6970   electronic ISSN 1554-6306   ISBN 0-7879-8528-7

The **ASHE Higher Education Report** is part of the Jossey-Bass Higher and Adult Education Series and is published six times a year by Wiley Subscription Services, Inc., A Wiley Company, at Jossey-Bass, 989 Market Street, San Francisco, California 94103-1741.

For subscription information, see the Back Issue/Subscription Order Form in the back of this volume.

CALL FOR PROPOSALS: Prospective authors are strongly encouraged to contact Kelly Ward (kaward@wsu.edu) or Lisa Wolf-Wendel (lwolf@ku.edu). See "About the ASHE Higher Education Report Series" in the back of this volume.

Visit the Jossey-Bass Web site at **www.josseybass.com.**

Printed in the United States of America on acid-free recycled paper.

Advisory Board

The ASHE Higher Education Report Series is sponsored by the Association for the Study of Higher Education (ASHE), which provides an editorial advisory board of ASHE members.

Contents

Executive Summary

The traditional sectors of public and private higher education are now joined by a newly prominent third sector: for-profit higher education. Although it is often discussed as a recent phenomenon, the for-profit sector has been a component of the educational enterprise in the United States since the early 1800s. Through much of their history, for-profits existed on the margins of postsecondary education, serving a niche market with short-term vocational programs. Today, however, the old association with matchbook cover advertisements for career training institutes does not do justice to the scope and diversity of for-profit higher education. Marked by the dramatic rise of degree-granting institutions and enrollment growth driven by large publicly traded corporate owners, for-profit higher education has entered the Wall Street era. A new type of degree-granting, shareholder-owned for-profit campus has grabbed the attention of the higher education community, with large multistate institutions like the University of Phoenix dominating the discussion of what the sector means for traditional colleges and universities.

The for-profit sector, however, is more than just the University of Phoenix. Many of the small schools operating in the nineteenth century still exist today. A range of degrees are awarded, from associate through doctorate. For-profit institutions are owned by public corporations, families, and venture capitalists. They operate in a single location or have campuses across the country. As the new dimensions of for-profit higher education in the Wall Street era continue to rise in prominence, it is important to clearly identify the variety of institutional types that make up the sector. A classification of for-profit higher education that distinguishes among institutions by degrees awarded, ownership, and geographic range usefully identifies the different elements of the sector and allows the identification and exploration of trends in areas such as corporate ownership, geographic variance, and the development of multistate institutions.

The public corporations that have come to define the Wall Street era of for-profit higher education have certainly changed the landscape of the sector. The implications of their growing influence, however, are uncertain. Three hypotheses are offered here. First, the growth of public corporate ownership has reduced the connection to the local community formerly maintained by the independent proprietary school. Second, corporate-owned institutions are increasingly positioned as narrow competitors to traditional higher education in cash-cow fields rather than niche providers for students ill served by conventional institutions. Finally, corporate owners have destabilized the sector by establishing a culture of growth that demands short-term returns to finance continued expansion. Although little is known about the impact of different ownership models on for-profit institutional practice, notable transitions are taking place that suggest the new corporate influence on the sector and its relationship to traditional higher education warrant close attention.

The diversity of the for-profit sector is evident not just in its organizational forms but also in the students who attend, the courses they take, and the academic models employed in their instruction. Enrollments in the for-profit sector represent fewer than 5 percent of the total postsecondary enrollment in the United States, but the for-profit sector enrolls relatively higher proportions of low-income and minority students than do traditional institutions of higher education. These proportions vary by degree level, however, with four-year for-profits less likely to serve large minority and low-income populations than two-year and nondegree institutions. Gender differences are evident as well, with women accounting for nearly three-quarters of the enrollment at nondegree for-profits, compared with a roughly even split between men and women enrolled in degree-granting institutions. The recent expansion of degree-granting institutions, then, has an impact on student diversity of the sector. Academically, vocational training remains a significant function across all institutional types, with programs in allied health, business, and computer technology among the most popular in degree-granting institutions. The number of degrees awarded has steadily increased, but even the new degree-granting institutions still award a substantial number of nondegree certificates. In terms of instruction, few for-profits offer tenure, research is rarely combined with teaching, and classes tend to be directed toward independent learners, conveniently scheduled year round. Yet it is not possible to identify a general for-profit academic model. Certain elements such as a centrally designed curriculum and a predominantly part-time faculty seem indicative of a few large corporate-owned systems. Some institutions that remain independent of corporate ownership, on the other hand, have more traditional academic models, including broad faculty responsibility for the curriculum. Unfortunately, information is limited about the range of academic models employed by the sector or whether their various components are common or rare.

The for-profit sector operates in a regulatory environment composed of the same state, federal, and accreditation triad as traditional not-for-profit private and public sector institutions. The general trend has been toward incorporating for-profits into a common state regulatory framework for all postsecondary institutions, regardless of sectoral affiliation. At the federal level, for-profit institutions are recognized under the Higher Education Act as a distinct sector, separate from not-for-profit private and public institutions, though proposals before Congress would eliminate that distinction. The Department of Education regulates those for-profit institutions that accept student aid (and most degree-granting institutions do). In addition, publicly traded institutions are under the regulatory authority of the Securities and Exchange Commission, and as business enterprises, all for-profits must answer to the Federal Trade Commission. Legitimate degree-granting for-profits almost universally hold accreditation, the third leg of the triad, though most are accredited by national agencies rather than the regional agencies that accredit most traditional colleges and universities. Still, regional accreditation of the for-profit sector is becoming more common since the first institutions achieved this status in the 1970s.

In the future, the remarkable growth of for-profit higher education is likely dependent on the fortunes of the large corporate owners that exemplify the Wall Street era. The sector has regularly seen cycles of growth and contraction, and a swing of the pendulum could return for-profits to the margins of the postsecondary enterprise. Certain elements at play, however, suggest a fundamental transformation has occurred. The amount of available capital for expansion is huge, the student market is growing, and the most prominent for-profits have achieved name-brand status. Higher education itself has changed as well, and the practical career-oriented education provided by the for-profit sector is increasingly valued as personal and public policy goals. Global trends toward privatization linked with increasing student access to education point to an increasing market for for-profit higher education. Even if the future is uncertain, however, it is clear that the assumptions of past eras are problematic when applied to the sector today. Better information is needed about these institutions, their owners, and their activities. The for-profit sector is currently playing an outsized role in the ongoing transformation of higher education. It is imperative that its growing influence be understood.

Foreword

Conversations about higher education tend to classify institutions as public or private or by type—research universities, community colleges, and liberal arts colleges. What is missing from this conversation is the for-profit sector of higher education. Despite their long-standing presence in the landscape of American higher education, for-profit institutions tend to be dropped from mainstream conversations about higher education policy and research. For-profit institutions operate on the fringe of higher education, and those who work in and study traditional forms of higher education—the public and private research universities, liberal arts colleges, and community colleges—tend to view them suspiciously.

Why is it that institutions in the for-profit sector remain on the fringe? One reason is that they have been overlooked historically throughout the evolution of higher education. Even though the concept of for-profit higher education has been around longer than Harvard, the tendency is to see for-profits as forever new. Another reason these institutions exist on the fringe is that they are hard to classify and understand. The for-profit category is expansive and diverse and by definition seemingly defies classification. The category includes everything from the large national chains of institutions (the University of Phoenix and DeVry, for example) to small single-entity institutions that offer specialized training in truck driving or culinary arts. The size and recent growth of the national chains of for-profit higher education tend to obscure the complexity of the category as a whole. For-profit higher education tends to be viewed synonymously with the likes of the University of Phoenix, and as long as this shortsightedness permeates mainstream understandings of for-profit higher education, the rich history and complexity of the for-profit sector will be regrettably misunderstood and left on the fringes of "real" higher education.

Kevin Kinser, in *From Main Street to Wall Street: The Transformation of For-Profit Higher Education*, remedies this obscurity by offering a historical overview of the for-profit sector that charts its growth and evolution from colleges in main street store fronts that offered specialized training to today's large and competitive for-profit institutions that have a presence on Wall Street. Kinser also offers a long overdue classification system that takes into account institutions' locations, ownership, and highest degree offered. Kinser's classification system is helpful as a heuristic to organize the for-profit sector as a way to be policy relevant and to be useful for further research.

The monograph has four main goals. The first is to offer the reader a historical perspective of the for-profit sector that charts the history using a framework of "eras" to chart the growth and diversification of for-profit colleges and universities. This history contextualizes the for-profit sector relative to mainstream higher education. The book's second aim is to explain and make sense of the diversity of for-profit institutions by offering the classification system mentioned above. This system offers those not familiar with for-profits an overview of the types of institutions in the for-profit category. The third goal is to summarize existing research about for-profit colleges and universities. A majority of the research related to for-profits mentions that little is known about the for-profit sector. Over time, however, a fair amount of research has been amassed about for-profit institutions, yet it has not been viewed systematically. Kinser masterfully reviews and synthesizes what amounts to a fair amount of literature on for-profits. The fourth goal of the book is to make a case for a "third sector" of higher education that can rightfully stand beside the traditional not-for-profit private and public colleges and universities. Such a classification will provide a more rounded perspective on what constitutes the totality and diversity of contemporary higher education.

This monograph is a must-read for those who want a more informed understanding of the diverse and ever growing for-profit category of higher education and its relationship to higher education as a whole. Kinser's work provides a foundation for further research and policy development regarding for-profit institutions and accordingly is sure to be of interest to those who study these institutions. The monograph is also a valuable tool for students of higher education wanting a comprehensive understanding of higher education in general and for-profits, in particular. This monograph should take a place on the bookshelves of all students, researchers, and practitioners of higher education.

Reading this monograph opened my eyes to the rich history and diversity of for-profit higher education. I hope that Kinser's comprehensive treatment of the for-profit category will help ground these institutions more firmly on the contemporary landscape of higher education.

Kelly Ward
Series Editor

Published online in Wiley InterScience
(www.interscience.wiley.com) • DOI: 10.1002/aehe.3105

Considering the Third Sector: The New Prominence of For-Profit Higher Education

OR NEARLY THE ENTIRE 350-YEAR HISTORY of higher education in the United States, nonprofit status has importantly defined colleges and universities. Rather than operating for private gain, higher education institutions were created to serve the public good. The two ways that institutions are funded in their service to society has been simply classified into either public or private higher education. Private sector institutions are primarily supported by nongovernmental dollars, including student tuition and fees, while public sector institutions are sponsored by the state through tax revenues. Adoption of this classification based on nonprofit status has proved useful for public policy analyses, historical treatises, and reform theses.

It unfortunately is incomplete. Whitehead (1973) has demonstrated how the early colonial colleges do not fit neatly into these categories: it was well into the nineteenth century before the modern definitions of public and private higher education took hold. More recent scholarship has shown how ostensibly nonprofit universities have entered the marketplace, for good or for ill, and now conduct a large portion of the academic enterprise with an eye toward the bottom line (Bok, 2003; Kirp, 2003; Newman, Couturier, and Scurry, 2004; Slaughter and Rhoades, 2004; Stein, 2004). Government support for public institutions is declining and their reliance on tuition and endowment increasing. The advent of six-figure tuition bills for a private college degree along with the decline of need-based student aid raise questions among critics as to whether higher education is operating for the public good or institutional aggrandizement.

Entering this blurred reality of nonprofit public and private higher education is a newly prominent third sector: for-profit higher education. These institutions are private, but they do not have the eleemosynary heritage of traditional non-profit higher education. They are not publicly supported through tax revenue, but the majority of their income comes from government subsidies of student tuition. They offer undergraduate and graduate degrees but only in a rather narrow range of fields. Many hold the same regional accreditation as their not-for-profit private and public sector cousins, though few offer a curriculum that has the depth and scope of a traditional college or university. Some are owned by individual proprietors, others by shareholders of multibillion dollar corporations, but all reject the claim that private gain trumps the broader service to students and society they provide. Unique and idiosyncratic as both a niche provider and alternative organizational form, these institutions exist well within the competitive framework that defines postsecondary education in the twenty-first century. The for-profit sector today exists in a higher education environment that has become increasingly complex, less sectorally distinct, and more diverse in terms of mission, function, and finance.

Much attention has been paid to the for-profit sector of late. Attention, however, has not translated into much understanding, nor even much of an effort to consolidate disparate strands of information about the sector—historical as well as contemporary—into a coherent picture of its scope and impact. Higher education mostly continues to be classified as public or private—even when acknowledging that dichotomy is insufficient—and the for-profit sector is only sporadically included in discussions of the postsecondary enterprise. What makes it all the more remarkable is the fact that for-profit higher education has existed along with public and private not-for-profit institutions since the eighteenth century. The sector has been eligible for public subsidies through tuition aid for nearly as long as traditional colleges and universities. And there exists an essentially unread literature on profit-making educational institutions that goes back a hundred years.

Each generation, it seems, discovers for-profit higher education anew and promptly complains about the lack of reliable information on the sector. Consider these statements:

The lack of a national "audit" of all proprietary schools affords an incomplete picture of our total national educational resources. (Miller and Hamilton, 1964, p. 260)

With debate about the purposes of higher education and the introduction of the phrase "postsecondary education," the proprietary school is being studied with renewed interest. The schools have long existed but due to lack of information negative connotations persist, especially regarding their educational merit or value to society. (Trivett, 1974, p. i)

We remind our readers that national data on this sector of postsecondary education are not easy to come by. (Carnegie Foundation for the Advancement of Teaching, 1987, p. 21)

Proprietary schools or, as they are sometimes called, "private career schools," are not well known or understood. . . . [A]cademic researchers in the education field have largely ignored the sector. (Lee and Merisotis, 1990, p. iii)

We cannot, however, present a complete picture of career colleges, because there has been limited scholarly interest in them and therefore limited data about them. (Clowes and Hawthorne, 1995, p. 2)

Despite widespread public attention and growing anxiety in some segments of the postsecondary enterprise, considerable confusion remains about the size and nature of the for-profit sector. (Bailey, Badway, and Gumport, 2003, p. 7)

Researchers have been investigating the for-profit sector for decades. A great deal more information is available than is generally acknowledged. Enrollment estimates can be traced to the 1870s. Curricular data have been published for institutions throughout the twentieth century. Substantial regulatory information exists from the 1950s to the 1990s. Information on student outcomes, faculty activities, ownership patterns, and accreditation standards can all be found in the literature on the for-profit sector. Still it is easy to claim that little is known about these institutions,[1] particularly in comparison with the well-researched public and private not-for-profit higher colleges and universities.

There are several reasons for this seeming lack of information. Probably the most important is that for-profit higher education has existed on the fringes of the educational system, associated more with matchbook cover advertisements offering a speedy road to a career rather than the hallowed halls of alma mater. Profit-making schools do not seem to be cut from the same cloth and so are often considered as separate institutions—if indeed they are considered at all. Another explanation is likely a reflection of the relative youth of higher education as a field of study. The focus of the research has tended to emphasize "higher," and nondegree institutions and other organizations outside the framework of degree-granting colleges and universities have received short shrift (see, for example, Adelman's report [2000] on the "parallel universe" of certification training programs). A third reason for the lack of sustained research about the for-profit sector is that interest in these institutions has been episodic, typically tied to exposing some perceived disreputable behavior or refuting allegations of the same. The clearest example of this interest is the flurry of reports, books, and articles in the 1970s concerned with the ability of for-profit institutions to participate appropriately in federal student aid programs (see, for example, Erwin, 1975; Hyde, 1976; Jones, 1973; Jung, Campbell, and Wolman, 1976; Shoemaker, 1973; Trivett, 1974; Wilms, 1974). The research and commentary faded as for-profit participation became routine. The next burst of attention came in the late 1980s and early 1990s with a wave of scandals in the sector primarily involving high student loan default rates (for example, Apling, 1993; Davis, 1994; Dynarski, 1994; Fitzgerald and Harmon, 1988; Grubb, 1993; Lee and Merisotis, 1990; Wilms, 1987). Despite the clear connection in the research questions between the two eras, almost none of the authors from the 1970s participated in the new analyses of the 1980s and 1990s. And when scandals over default rates lost their luster as a research topic, the for-profit sector once again dropped below the scholarly radar.

Why Now?

The for-profit sector is certainly on the radar screen today. Its new prominence has been triggered by a number of factors. Most significant, perhaps, is the 1990s expansion of for-profit institutions owned by publicly traded companies (Ruch, 2001). Even though, as discussed later in this volume, corporate owned for-profit institutions are nothing new in the United States and nationwide chains were well established as far back as the 1850s (Miller and Hamilton, 1964), the emergence of these new institutions seemed to catch the spirit of the times. As for-profit "universities" supported by the optimistic forecasts of stock market analysts opened across the country, *The Chronicle of Higher Education* began actively covering these institutions and their corporate owners (Strosnider, 1998), and commentators took note (Marchese, 1998; Winston, 1999). The corporate expansion became linked with two simultaneous occurrences: the rise of degree-granting for-profit higher education and the evolution of Internet-based distance education. The proportion of for-profit institutions offering degrees increased quickly after 1995, with major publicly owned institutions like DeVry, ITT Tech, and the University of Phoenix prominently represented in the expansion. Distance education, too, became important at the same time. With the establishment of a commercially oriented World Wide Web, technology became the "silver bullet" (Twigg, 1996) that would allow access to education to enormous numbers of new students at minimal cost. For-profit providers were seen as the natural exploiters of this new technology (Noble, 1997). Public corporate ownership of for-profit higher education became entwined with these developments. The old concept of a small proprietary school—owned by a local entrepreneur offering short-term career training in low-skill fields—gave way to a new understanding: a multistate corporate-owned institution offering degrees through distance education. For-profit higher education moved from Main Street to Wall Street, and the transformation has led to new reflections on a suddenly significant sector.

A decade into this latest era of for-profit higher education, it has become clear that the three trends need to be separated. For-profit higher education may be increasingly owned by public corporations traded on Wall Street, but there are still plenty of mom-and-pop proprietors running schools from a storefront in middle America—not all that different from the *Classrooms on Main Street* that Clark and Sloan (1966) wrote about in the 1960s. Degree-granting institutions may be ascendant, but the majority of schools in the for-profit sector do not grant degrees, similar to Hyde's *Metropolitan Vocational Proprietary Schools* (1976) of the 1970s. Distance education may be a growing phenomenon, but the for-profit sector is no more likely today to offer online opportunities than are public sector institutions (Allen and Seaman, 2004). The transformation of the sector is not universal; not every institution is the University of Phoenix. For-profit higher education is a diverse phenomenon in the twenty-first century.

In fact, the diversity and shifting nature of the for-profit sector make the current era so difficult to understand. The pace of change can be dizzying. In the first four months of 2005, two private, not-for-profit institutions were purchased by investors who in turn declared them to be for-profit enterprises. The reverse occurred at a for-profit college when the owner converted it to non-profit status. Career Education Corporation was the subject of a *60 Minutes* report that challenged the business practices of the publicly held company. Two privately held companies subsequently announced initial public offerings. Legislation was introduced in Congress that would eliminate distinctions between for-profit and not-for-profit schools in the Higher Education Act. The Federal Trade Commission began a consumer information campaign against diploma mills. And the University of Phoenix opened four new campuses. The for-profit sector does not sit still for analysis. Researchers today must take aim at a moving target.

Taking Aim

This volume has four main goals. The first is to establish a historical perspective on the development of the for-profit sector in the United States. In most contemporary writing, the phenomenon is treated with only cursory attention to the antecedents of the institutions seen today. Although much is new about the current era, much is familiar, too. And, as noted earlier, the for-profit sector has been described and documented for more than one hundred years. It is time to revisit that literature and make it part of the current record. The second goal is to emphasize the diversity of the for-profit sector. Too often, discussions of for-profit higher education simply recount the operating procedures of the University of Phoenix and similar large corporate providers. They may be dominant institutions in today's environment, but they are certainly not representative of the sector as a whole. Third, this volume serves as a summary of existing research and information available on for-profit higher education. It is not, however, intended to be comprehensive. The focus is more on questions relating to the organization and educational mission of the for-profit sector than on its economics. Finally, the overall purpose of this effort is to focus on for-profit higher education as a "third sector" of the higher education enterprise,[2] part of the same universe of institutions as traditional not-for-profit private and public colleges and universities. Significant scholarship has been devoted to the public and nonprofit private sectors, drawing out their distinctiveness and organizational idiosyncrasies. Similar attention should be paid to this third sector, with close attention to the variety of practices that fall under the label of for-profit higher education.

The Target

This volume is about for-profit higher education. Understanding the subject of interest, however, centers on what is meant by "for profit" and what sort of institutions count as "higher education." Neither concept is particularly clear-cut. How is it that a wealthy institution like Columbia University—with its billions in endowment, revenue-generating patents, and cash cow continuing education programs—is not considered a for-profit enterprise? And why should the Lia Schorr Institute of Cosmetic Skincare Training, a for-profit school located just blocks away from Columbia in New York City, be counted as an institution of higher education? The questions may seem abstract, but they concern what precisely should be legitimately included in the postsecondary universe and, by extension, serve to justify the perspective taken toward the for-profit sector in this volume.

The tax code defines the profit status of any U.S. organization. Not-for-profit educational institutions are known as 501(c)(3) organizations, after the section of the tax code that describes them. These institutions cannot be organized to benefit private interests, their assets must be permanently dedicated to charitable purposes, and net earnings cannot be distributed to owners or shareholders (Internal Revenue Service, 2003). The activities of for-profit institutions are not similarly restricted. They can operate with the sole intent of diverting excess revenues to their owners or shareholders and can dedicate themselves to the most uncharitable purposes imaginable. Data on the for-profit sector in the United States are collected by the National Center for Education Statistics (NCES) under a definition that describes these schools as "private institution[s] in which the individual(s) or agency in control receives compensation other than wages, rent, or other expenses for the assumption of risk" (2003a).[3] For-profit institutions, then, are distinguished from their not-for-profit peers not by their ability to make money on organizational activities but by what they are able to do with that money. Not-for-profit institutions can make money too—many, in fact, make a lot of money—but they can use excess revenue only to develop the organization and continue its charitable or other nonprofit objectives. In contrast, for-profit institutions can essentially do whatever they want with their money, including offering additional reward to their owners, dividends to stockholders, and reinvestment in completely unrelated activities.

The term "higher education" resists easy definition, as its connotation is just as important as its denotation. From an institutional perspective, higher education simply refers to where students go after secondary school. In international contexts, for example, higher education institutions are often logically referred to as "tertiary education." From a curricular perspective, however, higher education refers to collegiate-level instruction, thus excluding many noncollegiate institutions that nevertheless are legitimate destinations for high school graduates. The phrase "postsecondary education" emerged in the early 1970s as a way of including noncollegiate institutions in policymaking while preserving the emphasis on academic degrees and campus-based colleges and universities implied by the curricular perspective of higher education (Trivett, 1974). The distinction has not held up over time. The major federal legislation in the area, the Higher Education Act (HEA), includes as an institution of higher education nearly any accredited school that limits enrollment to students who have at least a high school education. NCES, on the other hand, identifies all of them as postsecondary institutions, regardless of whether they award one-year certificates or the Ph.D. degree. Moreover, states, accreditors, and the federal government delineate few restrictions on whether an institution can be called a college or a university as opposed to a school or an institute, meaning conventional nomenclature cannot be used to distinguish higher education from postsecondary education. One could attempt to enforce the collegiate-level emphasis on a definition of higher education, but the vagueness of that concept presents its own difficulties: How would one place the multiple missions of the community college, for example? Any decision on the matter is as likely to obscure as to clarify the issues involved.

Therefore, because of its widespread policy implications, a broadly inclusive concept of higher education as contained in the HEA is probably most appropriate when discussing the for-profit sector. As unsatisfactory to some as it may seem when talking about beauty schools and truck-driving institutes—and even many of the narrowly focused for-profit institutions that call themselves universities—higher education is the title of choice for this volume. The higher education institutions considered in this volume in turn follow the specific designation of for-profit status stipulated in the U.S. tax code. Even as some might argue that traditional nonprofit higher education has made its own Wall Street transformation over the years (Bok, 2003, for example), the profit-making activities of legally nonprofit institutions are not part of the analysis here.

The perspectives outlined above have a few qualifiers. In documentation of the for-profit sector before the 1970s, writers may have used definitions that were broader or more specific than the current practice. For example, private business schools of the nineteenth and early twentieth centuries were not all for-profit institutions, though the data suggest that the vast majority were (Miller and Hamilton, 1964). Nor do they represent all the for-profit institutions operating during the period (Bolino, 1973). Rather than attempting the impossible task of parsing historical data for information on profitability or alternative institutional type, statistics and other information from earlier eras are treated as representative of the sector even though they draw an incomplete picture. Second, in contemporary literature and discussions, the word "proprietary" is often used interchangeably with "for-profit," even though not all schools run by proprietors are necessarily for-profit. On the other hand, institutions were rarely labeled as for-profit before the 1980s; proprietary was then the term of art. The convergence of these two terms seems appropriate, however, and not much will be made of the distinction in this volume. Third, accreditation of for-profit institutions was often not important—or, indeed, even available—to institutions before the 1970s. Some authors discuss the accreditation status of the institutions they describe (Belitsky, 1969), while others do not (Clark and Sloan, 1966). Much like the information on for-profit status, these data are considered representative of the sector even as they admit imprecise summaries of the institutional population of interest. Fourth, the for-profit sector is generally described in this volume based on data collected by NCES beginning in the 1970s. Because this data collection is designed to capture institutions participating in Title IV programs, for-profit institutions that do not participate in federal aid programs are neglected. Finally, many for-profit distance education institutions are not currently eligible for federal aid because of an exception to the general definition in the HEA that excludes them. Accredited for-profit distance education institutions are included in this discussion where possible, though as a result of the recent emergence and lack of data on these institutions, a full discussion of legitimate for-profit virtual universities is not attempted.

Organization of the Volume

These four goals guide the thematic organization of this volume: a historical perspective is important, the sector is diverse, existing scholarship should be summarized, and the same basic questions should be asked of the for-profit sector as are asked of the traditional not-for-profit private and public institutions. To that end, the next chapter provides a general overview of the history of for-profit higher education, identifying the various stages of development of these institutions and establishing the markers of the current era. Following the historical perspective, the challenges of adequately describing the for-profit sector of today are discussed in terms of the variety of different institutions that fall under the for-profit label. A classification of the sector is proposed to highlight the dimensions of for-profit higher education that seem most relevant to the current era. The dominance of publicly traded corporations is the topic of the fourth chapter. Emblematic of for-profit higher education today, these Wall Street companies are in large measure responsible for the transformation of the sector and its new visibility.

The next two chapters address the teaching enterprise in the for-profit sector. First, the students who attend these institutions are discussed, and then the academic model and instructional practices are highlighted. They are basic elements of any educational institution, and the availability and quality of the information available on these topics is at the heart of the matter for the for-profit sector. Following this discussion are two chapters on the regulatory framework in which the for-profit sector operates. Accreditation agencies have become significant players in the for-profit world, and the impact of state and federal regulation in creating the environment where the sector now thrives is not often acknowledged. The final chapter emphasizes the current transformation of the for-profit sector and suggests a research agenda that will more fully incorporate an understanding of for-profit institutions as part and parcel of the larger higher education enterprise.

From the Beginning: Development of For-Profit Higher Education in the United States

The private commercial school offers a somewhat vague and complex subject for study; the facts when found are difficult of explanation. Though the origin of this school is of comparatively recent date, the place and time of its rise are disputed, for in its early period it left little or no formal history; the increase of these schools at a later time has been so rapid as quite to confuse one with the material available for study. Partisanship of private school men on the one hand, and prejudice against private commercial schools on the other, have but added to the difficulties of giving a satisfactory treatment to the subject. [Herrick, 1904, p. 177]

FOR-PROFIT HIGHER EDUCATION is often discussed as a new phenomenon. Although the for-profit sector as it exists today certainly has new dimensions, for-profit educational initiatives in the United States have existed since colonial times (see Exhibit 1). In fact, the College at Henrico, the first college in the American colonies, was proposed in 1617 as part of a revenue-generating scheme for the cash-strapped Virginia Company (Land, 1938; Wright, 1988). The funds raised for this early corporate effort at higher education were inauspiciously diverted for other purposes, and the institution never enrolled any students. Although it would take more than 200 years after Henrico for for-profit education to fully emerge in the United States, the history of these institutions actually begins in 1494 with the development by Lucas Pacioli of the Italian method of double-entry bookkeeping (Reigner, 1959).

EXHIBIT 1
Development of For-Profit Higher Education

Era	Years	Description
Formative Era	1494–1820	Individual instruction, first text books
Pioneer Era	1820–1852	First organized schools, curricular development
Expansion Era	1852–1890	Dominant role in business education, national visibility
Competition Era	1890–1944	Federal- and state-subsidized schools become primary providers of business education
Federal Student Aid Era	1944–1994	For-profit schools participate in federal student aid programs, regulation established
Wall Street Era	1994–Present	Publicly traded corporations drive the expansion of for-profit higher education

An analysis of sixteenth-, seventeenth-, and eighteenth-century textbooks (Reigner, 1959) identifies several examples of individuals in England conducting instruction in bookkeeping based on the Italian method. The first English bookkeeping textbook was published in London in 1543, and in 1588 the book was republished by "Scholemaster" John Mellis. The preface to this version acknowledges an earlier 1543 version by Hugh Oldcastle, who "taught the booke" in London (Reigner, 1959, p. 10). A 1635 text contains a letter to fellow teachers of bookkeeping as well as an offer by the author to instruct anyone in bookkeeping at his home. In the early 1700s, one-on-one instruction in bookkeeping began to evolve into English grammar schools that promoted a practical education for students who had no interest in the classical training common in the schools of the day (Hayes and Jackson, 1935; Reigner, 1959). In addition to bookkeeping, the basic curriculum of these academies included topics such as handwriting, "commercial" arithmetic, and French.

Reprints of the textbooks common in England began to appear in the American colonies in the 1700s (Reigner, 1959), presumably to serve the needs of local teachers of these subjects. Evidence suggests that business courses were taught in Boston as early as 1709, with English grammar schools appearing in New York City and Philadelphia by the mid-1700s (Hayes and Jackson, 1935; Seybolt, 1971). As in England, the curriculum of these schools was oriented toward "practical" subjects and was designed to give students the skills important to trade and commerce (Seybolt, 1971). By the turn of the eighteenth century, American-authored textbooks were being produced, and in 1817 what Reigner (1959) calls "the germ of the American business school" appears in a book called *The Student's Assistant* by James Maginness, a teacher in Harrisburg, Pennsylvania. In an appendix entitled "Observations on the Management of Youth for Conducting Them Through a Useful Education" Maginness writes, "Many people are mistaken about what it requires to constitute an education. How many young men have we seen coming from the colleges with their honorary degrees of Bachelor of Arts and Master of Arts without being masters of either art or science. It is not uncommon for boys to have an opportunity of jabbering here and there through a few classical school-books without learning to spell, read, write, or understand their own language as they should" [quoted in Reigner, 1959, p. 28]. Maginness's words reflect a frustration with the rigid college curriculum that was evident in other reform and institution-building activities in the early nineteenth century. In the familiar historical narrative, attempts by traditional colleges to reform their curricula toward more practical studies were quashed by the Yale Report of 1828, while only a few new institutions were founded—such as West Point in 1802 and Rensselaer Polytechnic in 1824—that directly challenged the classical curriculum monopoly (Veysey, 1965). Another sort of collegiate institution did emerge, however: the private, for-profit business college.

Who founded the first for-profit business college is debatable. The first advertisement was for a New York school operated by James Gordon Bennett in 1824 (Herrick, 1904). Bennett announced that he would open "an English classical and mathematical school for the instruction of young gentlemen intended for mercantile pursuits." In addition to bookkeeping, instruction was promised in "reading, elocution, penmanship, and arithmetic; algebra, astronomy, history, and geography; moral philosophy, commercial law, and political economy; English grammar and composition" (Herrick, 1904, pp. 178–179).

No evidence exists, however, that he actually enrolled any students (Reigner, 1959). In 1827, Benjamin Franklin Foster began teaching penmanship, book-keeping, and arithmetic at his school in Boston (Hayes and Jackson, 1935) and effectively established what would become the core curriculum of the nineteenth-century for-profit business college (Reigner, 1959). The school does not seem to have been particularly long-lived, however, and so should be con-sidered the antecedent rather than the ancestor of the for-profit colleges of today. That claim is best assigned to an institution founded by R. Montgomery Bartlett (Herrick, 1904; James, 1900). In 1834 he opened his first school in Philadelphia and then moved to Pittsburgh in 1835, ultimately establishing Bartlett's Commercial College in Cincinnati in 1838. It was the first use of the word "college" in connection with this new form of practical education (James, 1900), and his school remained in operation well into the twentieth century (Reigner, 1959).

Eras of For-Profit Higher Education

Many for-profit colleges and universities of today can trace their beginning to these early institutions of the 1820s and 1830s. The diversity of the for-profit sector, however, admits few generalizations. Non-degree-granting proprietary trade schools, for example, have a separate lineage, and their origin is less clear. They likely grew out of the manual training movement of the late 1800s (Smith, 1999; Venn, 1964). The first barber school was founded in 1893 by A. B. Moler in Chicago (American Colleges of Hairstyling, 2000; Jeffers, 2002); the cosmetology institutions of today are direct descendants of his original school. Correspondence schools originated in Europe in the 1850s; they jumped the Atlantic with the establishment of a private home study school in Boston in 1873 and the Correspondence University in Ithaca a few years later (Bolino, 1973). Today's for-profit distance education institutions owe a debt to the International Correspondence Schools, founded in 1901 and still operating in Scranton, Pennsylvania, as Thomson Education Direct. On the other hand, the numerous for-profit professional schools of the nineteenth century did not survive to have any substantial impact on the pro-fessional schools of the present. The development of for-profit higher education in the United States has followed multiple paths. Still, the nineteenth-century private business college provides the most direct connection to the for-profit sector of the twenty-first century, with more than one hundred still in operation today. From these original schools, historians of the sector have identified three distinct eras of for-profit higher education (Hayes and Jackson, 1935; Knepper, 1941; Reigner, 1959).

The first era has been called the "pioneer period" (Reigner, 1959), the "experimental era" (Hayes and Jackson, 1935), and the "formative era" (Knepper, 1941). At the beginning of the nineteenth century, the apprenticeship system was waning because of the increasing size of businesses, and individual instruction of new employees was both inefficient and insufficient to meet the need for trained office workers (Reigner, 1959). Because the apprenticeship system had for so long been the primary source for business education, people resisted the new methods. But by the 1930s, the new schools had begun to overcome this resistance (Hayes and Jackson, 1935). Lasting until the early 1850s, this era was marked by the establishment of the early private business colleges by individual entrepreneurs. Three separate subjects of penmanship, arithmetic, and bookkeeping began to be collected into single institutions, establishing a basic curriculum, while teaching methods developed from rote repetition to lecture introductions followed by practice (Knepper, 1941). By the end of this era, there were perhaps as many as twenty private business schools, mostly in major cities on the East Coast but also in New Orleans and St. Louis.

The second era has been called the "period of organization" (Reigner, 1959), the "monopolistic era" (Hayes and Jackson, 1935), and the "business college era" (Knepper, 1941). Lasting from the 1850s to the 1890s, the for-profit business college became a prominent feature of the American educational landscape and held a virtual monopoly on business education. Much larger institutions with national reputations and the corresponding popularization of formal business education—especially for teaching students how to use new technologies such as the typewriter and telegraph—were defining elements of the period. The growth of the sector was remarkable. In 1870, the U.S. Bureau of Education began collecting data on all levels of education in the United States, and "private business schools" were included in the institutional mix from the beginning. In words not too different from what might be written today, an 1873 report from the bureau stated, "The rapid growth of the schools and the large number of pupils seeking the special training afforded by them sufficiently attest that they meet a want which is supplied by no other schools in an equal degree. . . . Hence, it would seem that there could be no question of their utility and importance nor of their title to recognition and encouragement" [quoted in Knepper, 1941, p. 68]. From the estimated twenty colleges in operation in 1850, at least 250 institutions enrolling more than 81,000 students were operating in 1890 (Knepper, 1941, p. 92). In 1890 in comparison, about one thousand traditional colleges and universities in the United States enrolled just 157,000 students (Snyder, 1993). The for-profit business college of this time was clearly a significant institutional presence.

The rapid rise of the sector during this era was in large part attributable to the Bryant and Stratton colleges. In the early 1850s, Henry B. Bryant and Henry D. Stratton were students at Folsom Business College at Cleveland. In 1852 (or 1853 according to Herrick, 1904), they formed a partnership with James W. Lusk, a teacher of Spencerian penmanship in northern Ohio, and together they established Bryant and Stratton Mercantile College in Cleveland. They quickly began to branch out, in 1854 opening a second campus in Buffalo (which evolved into the current Bryant & Stratton system), a third campus in Chicago in 1866, and a fourth in Albany, New York, the following year. Other cities followed in swift succession: St. Louis, Milwaukee, New York, Boston, Providence, and Philadelphia (Reigner, 1959). By 1865 Bryant and Stratton had at least forty-four locations around the country (Knepper, 1941). Expansion was targeted for every city with a population greater than ten thousand. If a competing college were already located in a city, Bryant and Stratton would first attempt to buy the campus, and if that failed, they would open their own campus to drive the original owner out of business. Daily management of the campuses was handled by local managers, who were paid a percentage of the campus profits. The textbooks were uniform across all campuses, and tuition paid at one campus granted the student the perpetual right to attend classes at any other campus in the system. Annual meetings of local managers were held beginning in 1863, which led to the organization of the first association of for-profit educators, the International Business College Association.

The Bryant and Stratton model was in some ways a victim of its own success. The local campus managers became proficient at running a business college and chafed at having to give up a portion of their profits to Bryant and Stratton. In 1866 a revolt of the managers led to the dissolution of the chain, with most campuses becoming independent colleges (Herrick, 1904; Reigner, 1959). At least ten of these original Bryant and Stratton campuses are still in operation today, including the nonprofit Rider University, founded as a Bryant and Stratton campus in 1865 in Trenton, New Jersey (Ruch, 2001).

The third historical era has been called the "expansion period" (Reigner, 1959), the "modern era" (Hayes and Jackson, 1935), and the "subsidized business education era" (Knepper, 1941). At the end of the nineteenth century, the dominant role of the for-profit business college was eclipsed by publicly supported institutions. Public secondary schools and land-grant colleges developed new models of vocational and practical education that undercut the market for the for-profit business colleges. The for-profit sector was isolated from developments in the public sector, and contemporaneous accounts questioned whether these institutions could survive (James, 1900). But they did survive, taking advantage of enormous population growth in the first decades of the twentieth century to serve new students.[4] Between 1900 and 1917, for-profit business colleges increased steadily in both the number of institutions and student enrollment (Miller and Hamilton, 1964). Although remaining a strong and significant educational institution during this period, the sector was on the defensive. On the one hand, states questioned the schools' advertising claims and passed restrictive legislation. On the other hand, competition with other institutions was growing: they did not raise their standards quickly enough in response to high school vocational education, and as universities began to seriously offer business courses, the for-profit colleges had to fight to maintain their status as legitimate providers of a higher-level practical education (Knepper, 1941). In 1917 with the passage of the Smith-Hughes Act, publicly supported vocational education was firmly established. Enrollment in state-sponsored and federally subsidized vocational programs doubled in three years (Venn, 1964), and by 1923 with the passage of compulsory school attendance laws, the nineteenth-century for-profit business college model was in decline (Miller and Hamilton, 1964).

Various authors describe this last historical era as continuing to the time at which they write. Hayes and Jackson (1935) and Knepper (1941) emphasize the waning importance of the for-profit business college through the Great Depression, noting the defining characteristic of the time as the significant and continuing competition from the public sector. By the time Reigner was writing in 1959, however, the national economic trauma of the 1930s had been transformed into sustained growth, and federal support of education had become established public policy. The dividing line between these two assessments is World War II, suggesting a shift in the fortunes of for-profit education at that time. A fourth era, then, begins with the passage of the GI bill of 1944 and is marked by the involvement of for-profit higher education in federal student aid programs (Lee and Merisotis, 1990).

The GI bill marked a switch in the relationship between the federal government and for-profit institutions. Previous legislation focused on supporting and developing public education and treated the for-profit sector as an afterthought. This attitude was a point of contention for these institutions, and in the 1920s and 1930s, they lobbied for federal policies to recognize for-profit schools as legitimate institutions (Petrello, 1987). Their efforts did not have much effect, as even a wartime effort to train clerical personnel—the traditional market of the for-profit business school—was contracted to public schools and colleges (Petrello, 1987). The first drafts of the GI bill also did not include the for-profit sector, but as the mantra of veteran's choice dominated congressional debate, most institutional restrictions were lifted (Kinser, 2002a). For-profit institutions became eligible institutions under the GI bill and participated fully in the educational benefits offered to veterans. After 1952 requirements for maintaining eligibility in subsequent federal programs shifted toward institutional accreditation. The National Association and Council of Business Schools created the Accrediting Commission for Business Schools to satisfy these requirements, and in 1956 the U.S. Commissioner of Education officially recognized it (Miller and Hamilton, 1964). The National Defense Education Act of 1958 continued the requirements of institutional accreditation and provided the policy foundation for the Higher Education

Act of 1965. Ultimately the 1972 reauthorization of the Higher Education Act solidified the federal government's commitment to student choice in postsecondary education, with obvious benefits to the for-profit sector. Accreditation policies were affected as well, with regional accrediting agencies in the 1970s accepting for-profit institutions as members after years of resistance (Kinser, 2005d; Van Dyne, 1974). Achieving and maintaining eligibility for federal student aid programs became during this era almost a necessity for a degree-granting for-profit institution to remain viable. By the end of the 1980s, the easy availability of student aid allowed for-profit schools to compete on equal footing with the lower-cost public sector, finally eliminating the pricing disadvantage that began nearly a hundred years earlier when subsidized business education began.

The opening of federal aid to for-profit higher education was not a smooth transition. Scandals, fraud, and abuse dogged the sector, resulting in increasing regulation and external oversight of institutional activities. Accreditation was the first element of this new supervision of these "independent" schools (Miller and Hamilton, 1964), in part a reaction to the fly-by-night providers that took advantage of the GI bill–funded veterans but also a reflection of the more ambitious academic aims of the sector. The for-profit providers also became increasingly integrated into the state regulatory mechanisms, at first merely as business enterprises and later, after the 1972 reauthorization of the higher education act, as part of the education system with other public and private postsecondary institutions (Chaloux, 1985; Hamilton, 1958; Trivett, 1974). Investigations by government authorities became a regular feature of the for-profit sector, and institutional purges were the frequent result. GI bill–inspired clampdowns on fraudulent institutions caused many to shut their doors in the 1950s. Another wave of closings hit the correspondence schools in particular in the late 1960s and early 1970s. Investigations of student loan abuse of the for-profit sector reached its height in the late 1980s, and again large numbers of for-profit schools did not survive the scrutiny. Based on these latter investigations, the reauthorization of the Higher Education Act in 1992 finally established rules directed at the specific abuses of the for-profit sector. Among other issues, long-standing problems with high default rates were essentially solved, and new guidelines were established to rein in high-pressure recruitment practices traditionally employed in the sector. Independent no longer, the for-profit sector by the early 1990s had become a regulated industry as a result of its participation in federal aid programs.

The current phase of for-profit higher education represents a fifth era—the Wall Street era—marked by the new visibility of publicly owned corporate providers of higher education as the most prominent face of for-profit higher education. With the price differential between the for-profit and public sectors significantly reduced through federal student aid policies and regulation establishing a stable competitive field, corporations were poised to dominate a new growth-oriented for-profit sector. The 1994 initial public offering of the Apollo Group (owners of the University of Phoenix) represents the beginning of the era, not because it was the first public corporation in the educational field but because it epitomizes the new Wall Street focus of the sector. Corporations had in fact existed for years, typically purchasing existing for-profit colleges from the original owners and operating them as subsidiaries of the parent company. This trend began slowly in the first decades of the twentieth century (Miller and Hamilton, 1964), and by 1970 the corporation was a prominent organizational form (Belitsky, 1969; Doherty, 1973; Fulton, 1969). Writing in 1969, for example, Belitsky identified at least eleven corporations that own sixty-seven schools (p. 52). A few for-profit institutions started to expand outside local markets and, like the nineteenth-century Bryant and Stratton chain, opened branch campuses in other states. The Association of Independent Colleges and Schools noted, for example, the existence of corporate chain ownership in a 1987 report, though several "prophets" of the association suggested that a return to locally owned schools was imminent (Petrello, 1987). Few would make that prediction today, largely because the Apollo Group and other corporate providers in the 1990s showed that Wall Street can be kept quite happy with a growth-oriented educational model that achieves economies of scale and a business strategy that ensures students remain eligible for federal aid (Ortmann, 2001).

Despite the dominance of these publicly owned corporations, it is good to remember that they still represent a small proportion of the total number of for-profit institutions of higher education in the United States. They do, however, enroll about half of all students in for-profit degree-granting institutions and account for most of the organic growth in the sector. And not all public corporations are equal. The Apollo Group, for example, stands out. In 2002 the corporation enrolled 18 percent of all students in the for-profit sector and 26 percent of all degree-seeking students, and accounted for about one-fifth of all four-year for-profit campuses (Apollo Group, 2004; National Center for Education Statistics, 2003b, 2005)—contrasted with the smallest public corporation, EVCI Career Colleges, which notwithstanding the plural name, operates only one small institution in New York City. The rise of the corporate providers has not standardized the for-profit sector into clones of the University of Phoenix, even as the corporate ownership model is shaping current understanding of for-profit higher education (see, for example, Berg, 2005; King, 2004; Kirp, 2003; Pusser and Doane, 2001; Ruch, 2001; Winston, 1999). Just a decade into the Wall Street era, the impact of this new style of for-profit higher education is not known. But the expansion of corporate providers has placed the for-profit sector solidly into the mix of postsecondary options available in the United States.

The For-Profit Sector Today

The for-profit sector today includes about eight hundred degree-granting institutions and thirty-five hundred non-degree-granting institutions. Together they account for $6.2 billion in revenue, primarily through tuition payments from approximately 800,000 students (National Center for Education Statistics, 2004b, 2005). Dimensions of earlier eras are still much in evidence. The curriculum comprises a narrow range of subjects focused on business and trade skills. National chains of for-profit institutions dominate the sector. Competition comes from public and private not-for-profit institutions, with subsidized models showing the advantage in terms of student enrollment and public subsidies. The sector's reliance on federal student aid programs that began in the 1940s continues unabated. Its reputation is questioned, and it continues to struggle to establish legitimacy as a recognized provider of postsecondary education.

Unlike some earlier periods, however, there seems to be little doubt of the for-profit sector's survival. Even with a string of scandals in 2003 and 2004

(Blumenstyk, 2004; Kroft, 2005), stock prices are at near record levels. For-profit owners' political strength has been demonstrated in recent negotiations surrounding the reauthorization of the Higher Education Act (Burd, 2004; Kinser, 2004a), and enrollment in for-profit bachelor degree–granting institutions has more than tripled over the last decade (National Center for Education Statistics, 2004b; 2005). Although for-profit institutions are of minor significance in terms of overall numbers—representing less than 5 percent of the higher education enrollment and only about 20 percent of all degree-granting institutions—they currently play a major role in policy debates in Washington and portfolio discussions on Wall Street. And on campuses across the country, the for-profit sector has made its presence felt: faculty and administrators have seen the advertisements, watched the *university* signs go up at the interstate office complex, and in many cases decided to teach a class or two for extra money (Kinser, 2005b; Lechuga, 2003).

Still (especially compared with the extensive body of research on the modern university) the size, structure, and complexity of the for-profit sector remain obscure. Some of these details are being clarified by a new group of scholars studying the sector as well as by more extensive data collection by the federal government. The diversity of the sector continues to challenge researchers, however, as simple summaries often distort the institutional and programmatic complexity involved in for-profit higher education (Kinser, 2004b, 2005d). The current era, for example, though defined by Wall Street institutions, nevertheless continues to support a vast number of small, family-owned main street operations (Kelly, 2001). This complexity makes for-profit higher education interesting; the lack of current information makes studying it a challenge.

Institutional Diversity: Classification of the For-Profit Sector

FOR-PROFIT HIGHER EDUCATION is often discussed as a single entity without recognizing the huge amount of institutional diversity in the sector. Large, well-known institutions tend to be used as stand-ins for the entire sector, and generalizations about curriculum and academic models are made from a weak empirical base. The literature generally tends to underemphasize the diversity among for-profits and portray the activities of major corporate providers as representative of all degree-granting for-profit institutions (see, for example, Kirp, 2003; Morey, 2004; Ruch, 2001). This focus reflects the recent emergence and expansion of huge national chains of for-profit institutions such as DeVry University, ITT, and University of Phoenix. The scale of these institutions in terms of their national distribution of branch campuses and the numbers of students they enroll certainly justifies the attention. Just these three institutions, for example, have more than three hundred locations in thirty-eight states and enroll more than 320,000 students. Although such figures are remarkable, it is important to recognize that hundreds of other degree-granting for-profit institutions in the United States have markedly less impressive statistics. A classification of these institutions is needed to clarify the diversity of the sector and to provide an orientation for future research.

Several classifications of for-profit institutions of higher education have, in fact, been proposed. Early systems were quite simple, using a single dimension to distinguish among institutions. In its initial accreditation decisions in the 1950s and early 1960s, for example, the Accrediting Commission for Business Schools labeled institutions as "business schools" if they emphasized placement and training for employment and "collegiate schools" if their emphasis was beyond the purely vocational (Miller and Hamilton, 1964). Evidence for the latter classification was the inclusion of a specific general education curriculum. Of the two hundred ten institutions accredited by the commission, thirty-eight are classified as collegiate institutions. The vast majority of the institutions in existence were not accredited, and so the commission's classification is of a select group. Although such a classification would allow rather broad distinctions to be made among for-profit institutions, in the current era it has limited utility. Most accreditation commissions, including all the regional accreditors, the Accrediting Commission of Career Schools and Colleges of Technology (ACCSCT), and the Accrediting Council of Independent Colleges and Schools (ACICS), require degree-granting institutions to offer a program of general education. Based on U.S. Department of Education data, these agencies accredit more than 70 percent of all degree-granting for-profits (Kinser, 2005a). A general education curriculum is not a particularly distinctive characteristic of these institutions.

In another historical scheme, Fulton (1969) cites a 1966 study that classifies proprietary schools as "offering (1) preparation for employment, (2) instruction for a licensing examination, or (3) a combination of the two" (p. 1023). He argues that it is "odd" to make such a distinction because most proprietary institutions combine these functions, and he suggests that field of study is a more appropriate marker. Based on this distinction, Fulton (1969) divides the for-profit sector into two categories: business schools, which train office workers, and trade schools, which focus on occupations such as auto mechanics and cosmetology. Independently, Belitsky (1969) proposed a similar categorization, dividing the for-profit universe into the two categories of business schools and trade schools and then adding two categories to separate the large numbers of cosmetology schools and barber schools. Belitsky's tally using 1966 data showed trade schools to be the most numerous (three thousand institutions), followed by cosmetology schools (2,477 institutions), business schools (thirteen hundred institutions), and barber schools (294 institutions). Other curricular classifications were common in the 1970s, including one published by the U.S. government that grouped institutions by occupational type

(Trivett, 1974) and a nine-type classification based on vocational focus (Erwin, 1975).

As Lee and Merisotis (1990) note in their commentary on Belitsky's classification (1969), however, generalizations about institutions are difficult to make under a curriculum-based scheme. Proprietary schools offer programs that may change from year to year as new fields develop and old ones are discarded, and a static curricular classification would struggle to keep track of the movement. Moreover, the variety of programs offered in the for-profit sector makes it difficult to find institutional common ground without balkanizing the for-profit universe into rather small and ultimately insignificant pods. Lee and Merisotis (1990) suggest a modification of the curricular classification scheme that is based on accrediting agency rather than institutional program. They argue that policymakers are most concerned with accredited for-profit schools and that the membership of the major accrediting associations can serve as useful indicators of institutional type. Accreditation is important because it is the primary means by which an institution can establish eligibility to participate in Title IV programs for student financial aid. More than fifty recognized accreditation agencies cover fields from acupuncture to theater (U.S. Department of Education, 2004), and thirty-seven agencies have for-profit institutions as members. For specific programs, particularly for non-degree-granting institutions, the accreditation rubric provides a good approximation of curricular scope. For example, the National Accrediting Commission of Cosmetology Arts and Sciences (NACCAS) accredits about one thousand institutions, all of which seem to be similarly focused. Other agencies, however, do not have such uniform membership. ACCSCT accredits nearly the same number of schools as NACCAS but has a membership that ranges from culinary colleges to truck driving schools—even cosmetology schools are included. Although accreditation in general is an important public policy consideration, the concept of a curricular classification based on accrediting agency does not provide good resolution for the for-profit sector.

More recent classifications of for-profit institutions have avoided focusing on curricular area. Merisotis and Shedd (2003) developed a classification of two-year for-profit institutions as part of a larger study of associate degree-granting colleges. Using NCES data, they conducted a cluster analysis on a range of variables to determine which ones statistically demonstrated differences among the institutions. The analysis immediately eliminated two variables—geographic location and occupational focus—because for-profit institutions grant most of their awards in occupational areas and have campuses located in cities or surrounding urban areas. The remaining variables include instructional expenditures; percentage of first-time full-time degree students; percentages of minority students, adult students, and part-time faculty; and percentage of certificates awarded. Merisotis and Shedd (2003) identify two groups of for-profit institutions, career connector institutions and certificate institutions, based on the proportion of awards the institution grants as certificates. The categories are roughly equal, with 367 career connector institutions and 333 certificate institutions. Thirty institutions were not able to be classified under their scheme. Merisotis and Shedd (2003) determined that the certificate institutions have a higher proportion of first-time full-time students, have a lower proportion of part-time faculty, and enroll fewer students on average than do the career connector institutions. Certificate institutions also tend to offer more specialized training and include most of the cosmetology schools (though the authors are silent about where other occupationally specific schools fall in their classification). Despite the elaborate statistical analysis, the authors' classification of the for-profit sector is quite basic. In an important contribution, however, their larger classification of all two-year colleges provides an empirical justification for analyzing for-profit institutions separately from not-for-profit and public institutions. Ultimately, though, the division of the for-profit sector into just two categories seems to miss several important elements that are important in the for-profit sector today.

The Education Commission of the States (ECS) proposed a classification that was specifically designed to highlight the changing environment for for-profit higher education in the 1990s (Kelly, 2001). Focusing on degree-granting institutions, the for-profit universe is divided into three categories: enterprise colleges, supersystems, and Internet institutions. Enterprise colleges are locally oriented institutions owned and managed by an individual, family, or small corporation. They generally have fewer than five hundred students enrolled in a single campus or a small group of campuses, and they teach a limited career-focused curriculum to meet regional needs. Supersystems are described as multistate, multicampus institutions with stock that trades on Wall Street. They are growth engines of the for-profit sector, adding campuses in new regions and showing increased enrollment to meet the quarterly profit expectations of their shareholders. And Internet institutions are the virtual universities of the for-profit sector. They have no physical campus, deliver all of their programs over the Internet, and often have substantial international enrollments.

The ECS classification is important for several reasons. It highlights the diversity in degree-granting for-profit higher education by emphasizing the differences between enterprise colleges and supersystems. Because the current growth drawing attention to for-profit higher education is based in the degree-granting sector, a classification that emphasizes distinctions among these institutions is useful. ECS also defines large publicly traded corporate chains as a distinctive institutional type and pinpoints the organizational form as most indicative of the current era (Kelly, 2001, p. 30). Understanding these supersystems is vital to understanding the sector, and the ECS classification underscores their size and importance relative to other for-profit institutional types. Finally, it makes a distinction between virtual universities—Internet institutions in the ECS model—and other for-profit institutions. The growth of the for-profit sector in the 1990s closely paralleled the development of online distance education, and the two developments are often linked (Breneman, 2005; see, for example, Marchese, 1998; Noble, 1997; Winston, 1999). In general, ECS well represents the current status of the for-profit sector, and the classification names provide good shorthand descriptors for three major institutional types. Since its publication in 2001, the ECS classification has been referenced in the literature a number of times (e.g., Bailey, Badway, and Gumport, 2003; Floyd, 2005; Kinser and Levy, 2005); it was the only classification identified in an annotated bibliography of the for-profit literature published by the Center for Higher Education Policy Analysis at the University of Southern California (Lechuga, Tierney, and Hentschke, 2003). These references, however, use the ECS classification only as a descriptive device, not as a frame for empirical research. Even ECS has not attempted to use the classification to identify degree-granting for-profit institutions and categorize them by type. For most analyses, it seems the names of the ECS categories are more important than the institutions they signify.

Even as it makes an important contribution to the literature on for-profit higher education, the ECS classification has several drawbacks that will likely prevent it from serving a more robust role in future research. The key dimensions of the rubric distinguish between campus-based and Internet schools and between publicly traded corporate institutions and their privately financed counterparts. This classification should logically form a two-by-two matrix with four categories rather than the three that ECS proposes. Revising the classification, however, would subdivide Internet institutions, devoting half the system to the smallest group of institutions. Even in the grouping as it stands, the Internet category likely includes fewer than twenty institutions, compared with several hundred each in the supersystems and enterprise types. The classification causes some unusual groupings in its two largest categories. For example, Blair College, a small school with one campus of four hundred students in Colorado Springs, would be considered a supersystem because it is owned by Corinthian Colleges. On the other hand, Westwood College, an institution with more than two thousand students on eight campuses in California, Colorado, Illinois, and Texas, would be considered an enterprise college because it is a privately held corporation. The names and descriptions of these categories do not provide a close match to all institutions covered by the classification, though it is worth repeating that the ECS category labels nonetheless resonate with the current reality of for-profit higher education.

A New Classification

A classification of for-profit higher education should establish a reasonable number of mutually exclusive, policy-relevant, descriptive, and nonhierarchical categories from data that are available for all institutions (Merisotis and Shedd, 2003). In other words, the categories should create precise distinctions that are useful to policymakers without being evaluative or proscriptive. Two approaches to classification are a characteristics-based approach such as the taxonomic system used in biology to classify living organisms and an output-based approach such as the system used to classify industrial firms based on product lines (Bailey, 2003). Bailey (2003) argues that applying an output-based system to higher education presents several challenges, including specifying what "output" is to be considered most important in the analysis. As was seen in the curriculum-based classification approaches, other challenges include specifying curricular descriptions that can encompass the evolving and entrepreneurial nature of for-profit programs. Bailey (2003) concludes that a "parsimonious" output-based system would prove elusive. Evidence of this lack of parsimony is found in the U.S. Department of Education's Classification of Instructional Programs, which contains hundreds of categories (National Center for Education Statistics, 2002). Therefore, a classification of the for-profit sector should use a characteristics-based approach such as that employed by ECS (Kelly, 2001) and Merisotis and Shedd (2003).

The following proposed classification system for for-profit institutions of higher education draws on the ECS system (Kelly, 2001) and adapts the Merisotis and Shedd (2003) system to elaborate on the two- and four-year degree-granting sector. It does not include non-degree-granting institutions because there are so many of them relative to the other institutions that they require a separate system to distinguish them. The classification is directed toward accredited and U.S.-based institutions because so little information exists about international for-profit higher education (Kinser and Levy, 2005) and because accreditation in large measure determines what is considered higher education in the United States. The goal is to create a classification that will be policy relevant as well as be useful for further research.

Elements of the Classification

The classification has three main elements: locations, ownership, and highest degree awarded. Each element is subdivided into three parts, creating a multidimensional framework that encompasses all degree-granting for-profit institutions.

"Locations" refers to the number or geographic scope of campuses associated with the institution. An institution can have one or more campuses located in a single state, several campuses located in neighboring states, or a national institutional presence through a system of branch campuses or as a virtual university. Crossing state boundaries is an important consideration in the for-profit sector because it requires the institution to meet additional state regulatory requirements and because maintaining a national presence requires scalability to support the infrastructure demands of a large institution. In addition, regional accreditation is based on the assumption that geography is relevant to institutional practice and is challenged by multistate cross-regional institutions (Kinser, 2005d). Single-state institutions are identified as *neighborhood* institutions to suggest their local orientation. *Regional* institutions are located in a few neighboring states, and *national* institutions are more geographically dispersed or are virtual universities.

"Ownership" refers to the management structure of the institution. *Enterprise* institutions are owned by a family or an individual entrepreneur. *Venture* institutions are owned by independent private corporations that include non-family members in significant management positions. And *shareholder* institutions are owned by publicly traded corporations. The corporate dimensions of ownership are important because owners define the institutional mission. Shareholder institutions, for example, must have a mission that contributes to the quarterly profit demands of Wall Street. An enterprise institution, on the other hand, reflects only the owner's inclinations. Venture institutions exist in the middle, operating with limited external accountability but without the idiosyncrasies of family ownership.

"Highest degree awarded" refers to the level of education provided by the institution. *Institutes* offer at most a two-year degree, *colleges* offer a four-year degree, and *universities* offer programs that lead to graduate or professional degrees. As Merisotis and Shedd (2003) showed in their analysis of two-year for-profits, awarding an associate degree is a distinguishing characteristic of these schools. It is reasonable to extend that consideration to other degree levels.

Data on highest degree and location are available through institutional surveys conducted by the National Center for Education Research. Regional and national accreditors can often provide more up-to-date information on these items as well. Ownership is more difficult to ascertain. Because they are public corporations, shareholder institutions can be identified from a number of sources, but complete data on the corporate structure of venture and family institutions require analysis of state incorporation documents.

Types of For-Profit Institutions

These elements can be combined to form a typology of the essential organizational types in the for-profit sector, allowing the identification and exploration of trends in areas such as corporate ownership, geographic variance, and the development of multistate institutions. For example, a neighborhood enterprise institute would include MTI College, a family-owned two-year institution operating in Sacramento. This type of for-profit school has traditionally been the most numerous of degree-granting for-profit institutions. The large corporate-owned chains like DeVry University, ITT, and University of Phoenix are national shareholder universities. Unlike the ECS classification, these large, well-known institutions are distinct from the individual schools that are owned by educational management companies. For example, Bauder College in Georgia is a neighborhood shareholder institute owned by Kaplan. This type may become more numerous as for-profit educational management companies purchase neighborhood enterprise institutes. Alternatively, corporations may choose to link formerly independent neighborhood institutes under a common management structure and form new regional or national institutions. For example, Educational Management Corporation created national shareholder institute Brown Mackie College in 2004 from several neighborhood and regional institutions. It now has more than six thousand students across eighteen campuses in eight states (Education Management Corporation, 2004). Understanding the relationships among these types of institutions will do much to help track the development of for-profit higher education in the corporate era.

Table 1 provides an initial typology of degree-granting for-profit institutions based on Integrated Postsecondary Education Data System (IPEDS) 2002 institutional characteristics data on location and highest degree. Public corporate ownership was determined by Securities and Exchange Commission (SEC) filings. Because ownership data distinguishing enterprise from venture institutions are not readily available, these two categories are combined. This classification, then, includes 360 shareholder institutions or about 40 percent of all degree-granting for-profit institutions. Even the simple tally presented here shows how they are distinctive from enterprise/venture owned campuses.

TABLE 1

Typology of Degree-Granting Institutions

Type	Number of Institutions		Mean Enrollment (Full-Time Equivalent)[a]	
	Shareholder	Enterprise/Venture	Shareholder	Enterprise/Venture
Neighborhood/Institute	62	303	711	352
Neighborhood/College	26	46	1,206	622
Neighborhood/University	14	34	998	825
Regional/Institute	15	26	730	204
Regional/College	5	7	762	819
Regional/University	4	5	605	86
National/Institute	47	76	481	384
National/College	49	35	651	404
National/University	138	6	2,496[b]	1,014
All Degree Granting	360	538	1,189	410

[a]Data on enrollment from IPEDS 2002 Institutional Characteristics Survey. Shareholder status determined from SEC corporate filings. Includes branch campuses and non–Title IV participating institutions with IPEDS records.

[b]Mean FTE enrollment of national shareholder universities would be 1,889 if University of Phoenix Online (with more than 48,000 students) were excluded.

Four out of five neighborhood institutes, for-profit schools that offer associate degrees within a single state, are classified as enterprise/venture institutions. At the other end of the spectrum, nearly all the national universities, representing primarily the many campuses of Argosy, DeVry, and Strayer universities and the University of Phoenix, are shareholder institutions. Shareholder institutions are bigger on average than enterprise/venture institutions across all degree and location categories. Enterprise/venture institutions tend to cluster at the associate degree level, with institutes representing 75 percent of all schools in these ownership categories. Shareholder institutions, on the other hand, are distributed across degree types, with 34 percent institutes, 22 percent colleges, and 43 percent universities. Further analyses could be done relating these categories to accreditation status, curriculum, academic models, and other relevant features of the for-profit universe.

Continuing Difficulties with Classification

Classification of the for-profit sector remains difficult. New ownership often results in name changes, separate campuses combine to form new systems, and multicampus systems can have distinct degree programs, accreditations, and identities at each location. It takes an alert researcher to keep track of the developments. Still, classification is important, as the long history of attempts to describe the for-profit sector shows. The proposed classification is one more attempt, and even so it is incomplete because of the lack of data on ownership. Classification of the sector has other problems as well:

Because the sector as a whole remains opaque to detailed observation, it is difficult to know in advance which are the relevant factors to include in a classification. What is known is based on a relatively small number of institutions, which then tend to drive the items used in the classification. Classifications of the for-profit sector currently focus on shareholder institutions because data on these schools are more readily available. If more complete data were available for other institutional types, then additional or alternative categories may emerge that are now masked by the focus on Wall Street.

The vast majority of the for-profit sector comprises non-degree-granting insti-tutions. Even less is known about this segment than of the more familiar degree-granting schools. The only attempts at classifying these institutions have been by curriculum, but that method does not work particularly well with degree-granting for-profit institutions. A major taxonomic difference likely exists between the degree-granting and the non-degree-granting institutions that justifies two different classification systems. This assump-tion, however, should be tested rather than assumed. Again, the lack of data is a barrier.

Even in degree-granting institutions, a sizable proportion of nondegree cer-tificates is awarded. And most four-year for-profit institutions also offer the associate degree. The proportion of degrees awarded at each level may be more relevant to classifying the sector than simply tabulating the high-est degree. For example, within the highest degree category proposed above, half the universities and nearly all the colleges also award associate degrees, and 38 percent award nondegree certificates. These numbers sug-gest a complexity of degree level in the for-profit sector that has generally not been considered in current research.

Even though it is the best single source for detailed information on the sector, the limitations of the IPEDS data create further difficulties. For the pur-poses of a classification, the schools listed in the IPEDS data do not rep-resent the full universe of all for-profit institutions. Some are not included because only institutions eligible for Title IV funding are obligated to return NCES surveys. Institutions that do not participate in federal stu-dent aid programs can choose not to reply. Jones International University, for example, is a regionally accredited degree-granting for-profit institu-tion, but it is ineligible for federal student aid because it is a virtual uni-versity. It has no IPEDS record and is not included in tabulations based on this source (including in Table 1).

Another, more substantial issue is that by the time the IPEDS data become available to the researcher, it is more than a year out of date. The Univer-sity of Phoenix, for example, is listed in the 2002 IPEDS data (on which Table 1 is based) as having an enrollment of 129,000 students on forty campuses—substantially fewer than the 227,800 students and fifty-six campuses listed in the 2004 Apollo Group annual report. In the fast-paced world of for-profit higher education, the lag time between data collection and reporting is a real limitation of the IPEDS data.

A third issue is that the IPEDS data identify institutions of higher education in a way that is inconsistent with institutional accreditation. The UNITID variable in the IPEDS data may indicate a single campus, multiple campuses, or an entire institution. Accreditation, however, always refers to an institution, including all associated campuses. In most cases in public and private not-for-profit higher education, these two "definitions" of institution overlap exactly. The multiple campuses of the University of California, for example, have individual UNITIDs as well as their own institutional accreditation. The for-profit University of Phoenix, on the other hand, has forty UNITIDs in the 2002 IPEDS dataset that represent 121 locations (Apollo Group, 2002), but it holds accreditation from the North Central Association as a single institution, distorting categories based on geographic distribution. Eight individually accredited institutions, for example, are national shareholder universities in the 2002 IPEDS database, even as they are represented by 138 UNITIDs.

Because accreditation status is important to financial aid, it has been suggested as an important factor for the classification of the sector (Lee and Merisotis, 1990). But from the perspective of public policy, accreditation by any recognized agency provides similar benefits in terms of federal aid. Moreover, most of the primary accreditors of the for-profit sector have a rather diverse membership. Some organizational or academic differences, however, may be suggested by the details of the accreditation standards and requirements of the various agencies, particularly with respect to national versus regional accreditation. A comprehensive assessment of accreditation policy linked to the activities of the for-profit sector would be a welcome addition to the literature.

Despite the difficulties with classifying the for-profit sector, it remains useful to have an explicit organizing framework for discussing these institutions.

As a descriptive tool, such a classification is useful. As a research tool, it can provide a much-needed model for organizing information about the sector. For example, the data may imply that shareholder-owned education companies seek higher enrollments for their campuses and are more likely to expand across state lines and offer higher degrees. These assumptions can be tested empirically by seeing how the distribution of institutional types changes as publicly traded corporations expand and merge. Alternatively, one could conduct a study of faculty roles in the for-profit sector, comparing and contrasting across degree levels, geographic distribution, and ownership models. The size and influence of shareholder institutions, for example, can be balanced against the larger numbers of enterprise and venture institutions. The importance of degree competition with public and private not-for-profit higher education can be explored with a sense of the true scope of the academic offerings in the for-profit sector. By emphasizing the diversity of the sector, a higher-resolution picture of for-profit higher education emerges from classification-based research, and broad generalizations are qualified by the limits of institutional type.

Shareholder Owners: Defining an Era

SHAREHOLDER INSTITUTIONS REPRESENT a substantial component of the for-profit sector today and symbolize the defining characteristic of the current era. Twelve publicly traded corporations own degree-granting for-profit institutions in the United States.[5] These corporate owners of shareholder institutions, listed in Table 2, are required to report significant details about their operations to investors and government agencies, and they represent an important source of information about the sector. The history of corporate ownership of for-profit higher education demonstrates once again that the sector did not emerge out of whole cloth in the last decade of the twentieth century. Rather, the present model of shareholder ownership developed over time in reaction to market demands, government support, and regulatory intervention. At the same time, the Wall Street orientation of for-profit higher education clearly indicates the transformation of the sector from its earlier iterations and is the basis for why for-profits are so prominent today.

History of Shareholder Institutions

It is difficult to identify the first degree-granting shareholder institution. Ruch (2001) states that DeVry University was the only such school in operation in 1991, implying that its initial public offering that year was the first of its kind. Ortmann (2001) likewise identifies DeVry's public offering as an "early example" that other corporations followed (p. 293). DeVry, however, had spent much of the previous twenty-five years as a quite profitable subsidiary of the

TABLE 2
Shareholder Owners

Owner	Founded	Public	Market Value (Dollars in Millions)	Number of Locations[a]	Enrollment[b]
Apollo Group	1973	1994	$14,968	227	267,900
Career Education Corporation	1994	1998	$4,125	82	97,300
Concorde Career Colleges	1986	1988[b]	$109	12	7,700
Corinthian Colleges	1995	1999	$1,638	151	64,800
DeVry	1931	1991[c]	$1,161	76	55,000
Education Management Corporation	1962	1996	$2,338	67	58,800
EVCI Career Colleges	1997	1999	$115	5	2,800
ITT Educational Services	1963	1994[c]	$2,134	77	42,200
Kaplan Higher Education	1940	1996[d]	N/A	70	45,000
Laureate	1979	1993	$2,165	43	155,000
Strayer	1892	1996	$1,683	30	23,000
Universal Technical Institute	1965	2003	$996	29	13,000

NOTE: Data for this table are drawn from corporate SEC filings and company Web sites.
[a]Includes campuses, distance education operations, and branch centers.
[b]Precise figures not available for all institutions. Enrollment is rounded to the nearest 100.
[c]Date is of first independent initial public offering. The company was previously a subsidiary of a public company.
[d]Date of EMI/Quest initial public offering.

40

Bell and Howell corporation, which purchased the school in 1966. DeVry was a well-known degree-granting institution, regularly referenced as a key example of the for-profit sector of the late sixties and early seventies (see, for example, Doherty, 1973; Fulton, 1969), much as the University of Phoenix is cited a quarter century later. The institution was sold to private investors in 1987 as part of a leveraged buyout of the parent corporation. So in 1991, when Ruch (2001) and Ortmann (2001) start the clock on the story of Wall Street and for-profit higher education, DeVry was returning to familiar territory. The DeVry public offering was a marker in the history of for-profit higher education, but it was not the first shareholder institution.

Nor was DeVry the only publicly traded institution in 1991 as Ruch (2001) suggests. Corporations have owned for-profit companies since at least the 1930s (Miller and Hamilton, 1964), though it is not clear whether they are publicly owned companies. By the 1960s, the ownership of for-profit institutions by public companies is noted as a "new dimension" of the sector, with a 1965 Bank of America study cited as proof of the investment potential of proprietary schools (Fulton, 1969). Fulton lists Bell and Howell and the Lear-Seigler Corporation as examples. Trivett (1974) cites several studies in his monograph that show a proportion of for-profit institutions are corporate subsidiaries, naming Minneapolis-Honeywell and Ryder Systems in addition to Bell and Howell as owners. In his comparison of public and for-profit vocational training, Wilms (1974) notes that a large public corporation sold one of the institutions in his sample shortly after the study was completed. A comprehensive study of proprietary schools in Chicago (Hyde, 1976) found that nearly one-quarter of the institutions were subsidiaries of a parent corporation, "chiefly those whose primary business is other than education" (p. 8). Williams and Woodhall (1979) note that public corporations owned about 5 percent of the sample institutions in their international study of for-profit education and echo Hyde's observation (1976) that the parent corporation is not itself principally in the business of education. Looking back on that era, Petrello (1987) also names LTV Aerospace Company, the Life Insurance Company of Virginia, and General Electric as corporations participating in a 1960s trend of diversifying into the for-profit education sector.

As the focus of most studies of the for-profit sector during this time was on vocational training programs and not all authors name the corporate owners, it is unclear how many of the corporate-owned schools grant degrees. Apart from Bell and Howell's DeVry, however, at least two other degree-granting shareholder institutions in existence today can be identified dating from the 1960s: ITT Technical Institutes and the Katharine Gibbs School. Bolino (1973) credits International Telephone and Telegraph with operating thirty schools that train students in technical fields, business, and fashion, the forerunner of today's ITT Technical Institute. He also notes that the Macmillan corporation "earns a good profit" from the Katharine Gibbs School (p. 171), a degree-granting institution now owned by Career Education Corporation. Both ITT and Katharine Gibbs were purchased by their parent companies in 1966, so not only was DeVry not the first shareholder institution in 1991, it also cannot hold claim to being the first in the 1960s.

All these companies were drawn to the sector by the lure of growing federal investment in education. Running proprietary schools was generally considered a profitable business (Hyde, 1976; Trivett, 1974), and capital development rather than educational development was the goal. Diversified corporate ownership, however, did not prove to be a stable organizational form. The 1972–73 recession and government investigations of fraudulent practices in the sector caused many corporations to rethink the value of their holdings. Some were sold to private investors or local managers, much as happened with the dissolution of the old Bryant and Stratton chain a century earlier. But for others, a different sort of corporation was waiting in the wings: a "pure-play" education company called National Education Corporation (NEC).

Unlike the diversified public corporations that had been operating for-profit institutions as subsidiaries, NEC had education as its primary business (Merwin, 1981). Founded in 1954 and taken public in 1961, the corporation started as a small mail order business and then expanded into home-study correspondence education. In 1968, NEC acquired its first campus-based school, and after narrowly escaping bankruptcy in the early 1970s (Merwin, 1981), the company went on a buying spree, snapping up weaker competitors and bidding for the for-profit school holdings of much larger corporations. By 1980 NEC was trading on the New York Stock Exchange. Among the few remaining multicampus owners of for-profit institutions, it owned as many as eighty-nine schools with revenues of $100 million ("Growth Cum Laude," 1981; "National Education: A Leader in a New Growth Industry," 1980). It tripled its revenues over the next five years (Wilms, 1987), continuing to be aggressive in acquiring existing for-profit schools, including degree-granting institutions: at one point, NEC attempted to buy DeVry from Bell and Howell (Dorfman, 1984). Through the 1980s, NEC was the largest provider of for-profit education in the United States, dominating the market and attracting glowing notice from sector analysts (Mendes, 1988). It was the University of Phoenix of career schools, in essence the opening act for the Wall Street era of the 1990s.

In addition to NEC, other for-profit education companies emerged as well, most taking advantage of an encouraging economy and regulatory environment to quickly expand their operations. A few large corporations spun off their education divisions as independent entities, turning subsidiaries into new publicly traded education companies. A computer firm, National Technical Systems, for example, owned twelve schools in California. In 1985, they were spun off into a new company called United Education and Software, and in three years it had expanded to thirty-three schools in ten states. Others were education companies that, like NEC, had been small public corporations for years and now started to grow by acquiring competitors. A good example is American Training Services, a truck-driving school operator since the 1960s. It was renamed Educom in 1981 and expanded into areas ranging from business to computer programming to medical technology. Operating under the name Careercom for the latter half of the 1980s, it owned eighty schools by the end of the decade. A third category is represented by Wilford American Educational Corporation, which emerged from a small chain of beauty schools in operation since the 1940s. It went public in 1984 and became a large holding company for cosmetology and secretarial schools across the United States. The final type of for-profit corporate owners during this period was newly founded education companies that quickly went public to finance new acquisitions. Canterbury Educational Services, for example, was founded in 1981 as a company offering one-day seminars. It went public a few years later and started buying vocational schools offering programs in truck driving, business, and medical services. These corporations signify the shift in the 1980s from public ownership of for-profit institutions as subsidiaries of large diversified corporations to public ownership by pure-play education companies. As the leader in the field, NEC broke new ground as a major public corporation focused on becoming a leading player in the for-profit educational market, and it set the stage for DeVry's reemergence as a public corporation in 1991 and ultimately the beginning of the Wall Street era.

What happened to all these companies? In many cases, accusations of fraud caused their stock to plummet, throwing the companies into bankruptcy or making them ripe for takeover. Careercom was investigated for student loan fraud in 1988, and by 1990 its eighty-campus system was for sale. There were no takers, so the company sold or closed half its campuses by 1992 to survive. Another investigation of loan fraud hit in 1995, and the company was finished. United Education and Software had a similar story. Student loan problems began in 1989, and the company hired a former U.S. Department of Education official to manage government relations. The company could not overcome its problems; it declared bankruptcy in 1990 and had sold all its assets by 1994. Other companies had problems with the SEC related to their accounting practices or suits from shareholders arising from misleading company statements regarding potential for growth. The reputation for shady practices in the sector left no reservoir of good will, and when scandal hit, the companies found it impossible to continue.

Because it was the biggest, the story of NEC is illustrative. In 1990, after a decade of solid growth and profits, the $450 million company suddenly posted a loss. The chief executive officer who had engineered the company's expansion was fired, and the shareholders sued, alleging they were kept in the dark about NEC's true financial situation. The collapse of the company was swift as it began selling off its campus-based schools to stop the losses and restore shareholders' confidence. By 1995, a group of former executives formed a separate company, Corinthian Colleges, and purchased the remaining sixteen schools in NEC's portfolio. NEC restyled itself as an educational publishing and corporate training company and recommitted itself to developing its one remaining educational institution, the International Correspondence School. It evidently was successful, because in 1997 a bidding war broke out between Sylvan Learning and Harcourt General over the company, with Harcourt eventually paying $720 million for all NEC's outstanding stock. The remnants of NEC's decade-long dominance of for-profit higher education can be seen in the core of Corinthian Colleges' expansion over the last decade as well as in the frequent television advertisements of NEC's old International Correspondence School, now a distance education institution known as Thomson's Education Direct.

Clearly, then, DeVry was not the first, nor was it the only, shareholder institution in 1991. Other degree-granting institutions were owned by publicly traded corporations since the 1960s, with pure-play education companies such as NEC beginning to own those schools in the 1980s. DeVry is not distinctive in the history of shareholder institutions, though it does represent a convenient marker for the growth of corporate-owned, degree-granting, for-profit higher education in the 1990s. DeVry was the first for-profit institution to go public as a stand-alone degree-granting college, and it initiated the steady and continuing growth in the number of shareholder institutions in the United States (Ortmann, 2001). With the exception of Concorde Career Colleges, all the current public corporations involved in for-profit higher education went public after DeVry, and those public companies that operated in the sector before DeVry are no longer active in for-profit higher education.

Current Owners

Much like for the education companies that came before them, development of the twelve corporations active in for-profit higher education today is a complicated story. As new corporations emerged, old corporations were subsumed, and formerly independent institutions came under a growing corporate umbrella. As Table 2 shows, together they own 869 campuses with an enrollment of more than 800,000 students. The diversity of this group of shareholder owners mimics the diversity of the sector as a whole. The largest, Apollo Group, has well more than one hundred times the market value of the smallest, Concorde Career Colleges. The oldest, Strayer, was founded more than one hundred years ago, while the newest, EVCI, was started in 1997.

Some, like Educational Management Corporation, own huge multicampus chains. Others, like Kaplan, focus more on individual campuses. Most focus their activities in the United States and Canada, but Laureate is unique in the extent of its international holdings.

Because of the variety with which shareholder owners approach their business, it is difficult to speak generically about them as a group. It is good to remember as well that they are each other's biggest competitors, with business plans designed to gain advantage or carve out a niche to maximize profit. Growth strategies vary as well, with some corporations preferring organic development of their name brand and others seeking acquisitions in favorable markets. Although a full discussion of business plans and growth strategies is beyond the scope of this volume, a sense of the history and range of current corporate players as well as the regulatory and legal issues that each has faced gives a useful layer of context for the current Wall Street era. A brief overview of each corporation that owns shareholder institutions follows.

Apollo Group

Apollo Group is easily the biggest public corporation involved in for-profit higher education. Alone it has almost half the total stock market value of the sector, enrolling a third of the students in publicly owned institutions. Its current size notwithstanding, it had a rather modest beginning (Sperling, 2000). In 1973 John Sperling established an adult education program called the Institute for Community Research and Development that was based on his experience teaching police officers as a humanities professor at San Jose State University. That company developed into the Institute for Professional Development (IPD), which contracted with private nonprofit degree-granting institutions to provide adult education programs. In 1977 IPD established the University of Phoenix (UOP) in its bid to win regional accreditation. Sperling combined IPD and UOP in 1981 to form the Apollo Group and made the success of UOP the top corporate priority, while IPD continued to offer adult programs under contract with private nonprofit degree-granting colleges (Sperling, 2000). During the 1980s, the Apollo Group focused on developing and expanding the degree-granting

UOP, and after more than a decade of steady growth, the Apollo Group went public in 1994 at $8.25 per share.[6]

It proved to be a good investment. At the time of the 1994 initial public offering, the Apollo Group had locations in eight states, enrolling 27,469 students at thirty-three UOP campuses and twenty-seven IPD sites. A small distance learning operation enrolled about two thousand students. In ten years, the Apollo Group had more than two hundred locations in twenty-nine states and Puerto Rico and international operations in British Columbia, India, China, Mexico, and the Netherlands. UOP alone serves 228,000 students, including more than 100,000 in the online division, and has more than 150 locations in the Unites States and Canada. Apollo stock trades at more than $80 a share, and UOP Online (a tracking stock[7] for UOP's distance education division) grew from $14 at its initial offering in 2000 to $94 a share in 2004 when it was reabsorbed into the Apollo Group. The growth has been driven by UOP's expansion. IPD continues to offer contract programs with a limited number of private colleges and universities, and in its history, the Apollo Group has acquired only two institutions: Western International University (WIU) in 1995 and the College of Financial Planning (CFP) in 1997. Together, IPD, WIU, and CFP account for just 10 percent of the current enrollment in the Apollo Group and only 5 percent of the enrollment growth since 1994.

A few problems have accompanied Apollo's decade-long expansion. In the late 1990s, some questions were raised by UOP's accreditor, the North Central Association, about how the school counted student attendance and credit hours. In 2003 and 2004, questionable recruiting practices and student loan awards led to a rather critical Department of Education report and a large fine against the company. The company's failure to immediately disclose the contents of the report resulted in a lawsuit by shareholders that is still pending. Although they represent troubling issues for the Apollo Group and have certainly affected the value of its stock, the company as a whole has been relatively unaffected and continues to expand apace. Plans for 2005 include opening nine new UOP campuses, including a branch in Mexico; establishing new degree programs in education, business, and health; and developing a new undergraduate program for traditionally aged students at WIU called Axia College.

Career Education Corporation

The Career Education Corporation (CEC) is another large corporate owner of for-profit institutions, but it has a substantially different history and growth strategy from the Apollo Group. Founded in 1994 by John M. Larson, the company was established to acquire existing schools. This tactic is not surprising, given that Larson is a former executive of NEC and Phillips Colleges,[8] two companies that had similar expansion strategies in the 1980s. CEC began with two graphic design schools and quickly added others. By the time of its initial public offering in 1997, CEC owned eighteen campuses in thirteen states and Canada and served more than 13,000 students.

Investors grabbed shares at the $16 offering price, and the company used the infusion of cash to keep growing. It purchased the Katharine Gibbs Schools from an investment firm in 1997, and in a takeover of EduTrek International in 2001, the five-campus American Intercontinental University system was added to the CEC fold. Two more major purchases occurred in 2003. CEC absorbed the Whitman Education Group, with twenty-two schools in thirteen states, and INSEEC, a French company with nine campuses. But it was not just these big acquisitions fueling CEC's growth. It almost continuously purchased small campuses, and by the end of 2004, ten years after the initial public offering, CEC owned eighty-two campuses in twenty-five states, the United Kingdom, France, the United Arab Emirates, and Canada. Its acquisition strategy maintained the individual identity of the schools, keeping their original names rather than developing a nationwide system of institutions under a common brand. Consequently, CEC manages thirty separate schools with from one to nineteen campuses for each. Most are degree-granting institutions in the fields of information technology, visual communication and design, business, health, and culinary arts.

With the expansion came a series of scandals, investigations, and lawsuits. The Whitman purchase started it, with accusations of loan fraud at the newly acquired schools. Shareholders sued in 2003 and 2004, alleging misrepresentation of the corporation's enrollment and continued potential for growth. Accreditation difficulties followed, with two regional associations, the Western Association of Schools and Colleges and the Southern Association of Colleges and Schools, each independently questioning the corporation's top-down strategy of managing certain schools. At the same time, SEC opened an investigation of the company's public statements and accounting, and the Department of Justice seated a grand jury to hear further testimony about outright fraud in student recruitment and graduation policies. All the attention led to a *60 Minutes* exposé, where in classic investigative journalism style, hidden cameras exposed fraudulent statements and activities of several CEC campus representatives (Kroft, 2005). It is remarkably similar to the collapse of many for-profit education companies in the 1980s, including Larson's former employers, the NEC and Phillips Colleges.[9] At this point, however, CEC is holding its own, with stock prices climbing back to around $40 after being down as much as 60 percent from its high of $70 in 2004. After the Apollo Group, it is the second biggest company in the sector in terms of market value, and, with acquisitions ongoing, CEC remains a significant player in for-profit higher education.

Concorde Career Colleges

Concorde became an independent public company in 1988, making it the longest-operating pure-play corporation currently involved in degree-granting higher education. It got its start as a division of Cencor, an insurance and financial services firm that diversified into training for certified public accountants (CPAs) in the 1970s. In 1986 Cencor grouped its growing education holdings into the Concorde division and in 1988 spun off the division's nineteen institutions and CPA review programs as Concorde Career Colleges. It began active trading on the NASDAQ exchange in 1989 at $4.50 per share and almost immediately began struggling. It skirted bankruptcy in the early 1990s, was delisted from NASDAQ for share prices below $1, and was targeted by regulators for having high default rates at several of its campuses. By 1993 the Department of Education questioned the company's financial viability and therefore its participation in Title IV financial aid programs.

Concorde sold or closed unprofitable campuses and aggressively attacked the loan default problem. The company was reduced from a high of twenty-two campuses in 1990 to twelve in 1996 but had turned the financial corner. New investment came from venture capitalists in 1997, stabilizing Concorde's financial picture. Also at that time, the company shifted to a focus on degree-granting institutions, selling its CPA review business and upgrading the programs on its remaining campuses. Concorde stuck with its stable of campuses through the rest of the decade and into the 2000s, dropping one campus and acquiring one other. In 2002 it returned to NASDAQ trading at around $9 per share. Two years later, with stock prices above $25 per share, it began looking to grow again slowly from its current twelve campuses in seven states. With the smallest capitalization of the public companies involved in the for-profit educational sector, however, any expansion will come against much larger competitors.

Corinthian Colleges

Of all the public corporations currently operating in the for-profit higher education sector, Corinthian Colleges can best lay claim to being the successor to the pure-play companies of the 1980s. It was founded in 1995 by former executives of the NEC, who purchased sixteen schools from the collapsing corporation. A year later, Corinthian snapped up eighteen campuses of the faltering Phillips Colleges chain. With these schools as its core, the company went public in 1999 at $18 a share, having thirty-five colleges in sixteen states serving almost 16,000 students. The growth strategy of the company continued unabated, often purchasing campuses from struggling companies and turning them around to profitability and regulatory compliance. New campuses are created as branches of successful locations, and similar institutions are combined into broad regional or national systems under the same name.

Corinthian is organized into five divisions. The Corinthian Schools division runs forty-six schools that offer diploma and certificate programs in health care fields. The Rhodes Colleges division operates nineteen associate degree–granting colleges, offering training in health, business, criminal justice, and information technology. The University division comprises Florida Metropolitan University and the National Institute of Technology, two schools that offer four-year degrees on fourteen campuses in Florida. In 2003 Corinthian purchased the Canadian education company CDI and divided its operations into two new divisions: CDI Education, which hosts forty-five campuses of CDI College, and the Corporate Training division, which includes the fifteen CDI Career Training institutes as well as the operations of two Learning Tree University sites in California (also acquired in 2003). At the end of 2004, fewer than ten years after its founding, Corinthian was serving 64,800 students on 151 campuses in twenty-two states and seven Canadian provinces.

Like several other for-profit education companies, Corinthian faced regulatory scrutiny in 2003 and 2004. The Department of Education investigated one of its campuses for student loan violations, SEC opened an inquiry into potentially misleading statements made by the company about its status with the loan program, and several shareholder lawsuits erupted in the wake of these revelations. The president and chief operating officer quit in April after fewer than eighteen months on the job, leading to some speculation that under the smoke was plenty of fire. The stock took a nose dive, dropping to $10 a share from a high of $36 before recovering on news that the Department of Education investigation and SEC inquiry both closed with no penalties. Even so, at the beginning of 2005, several shareholder lawsuits remained to cloud Corinthian's future. The company is seeking to continue its growth strategy through acquisitions and by opening branch campuses—each of which requires approval from accreditors and Department of Education officials—so regulatory issues will likely remain a constant issue.

DeVry

DeVry, Inc., is the parent company of DeVry University, a regionally accredited national shareholder university, and Ross University, a medical and veterinary school in the Caribbean that DeVry acquired in 2003. The DeVry name originated in 1931 with the founding by Herman DeVry of a mail order electronics school in Chicago. Eventually, the movie camera firm Bell and Howell purchased DeVry's institute as part of a diversification strategy in the 1960s. As a subsidiary of Bell and Howell from 1966 to 1987, DeVry expanded from two campuses in Chicago and Toronto to eleven campuses in eight states and Canada. The current corporation, DeVry, Inc., originated with two former instructors at DeVry, Dennis Keller and Ronald Taylor, who in 1973 founded the Keller Graduate School of Management. They purchased their former employer from Bell and Howell in 1987 and revamped its curriculum to match the night school, part-time student model that had made Keller Graduate School successful. The new owners combined their eight campus graduate school with DeVry to form DeVry, Inc., taking the company public in 1991 at an initial offering price of $10 per share.

DeVry expanded steadily in the 1990s, with Keller Graduate School and the DeVry institutes forming two national chains. DeVry and Keller grew from a total of nineteen campuses and 25,000 students in 1991 to sixty-three campuses and 55,000 students in 2001. In 2002 the company reorganized Keller Graduate School and the DeVry Institutes into DeVry University, creating a single accredited institution. DeVry University now has seventy-three locations in twenty-one states and Canada, and the purchase of Ross University in 2003 added three more locations in Miami and the Caribbean. Unlike the other publicly owned companies, however, DeVry has not seen steady enrollment growth in the 2000s. Even with the addition of new campuses since 2001, current enrollment remains around 55,000 students. It showed the weakest revenue growth of the major public companies in higher education (*Chronicle of Higher Education*, 2004) and was the subject of takeover rumors in late 2004. Although it has remained free of any substantial scandals or legal tussles, its relatively low stock price of $16.50 per share makes it a good case study of how Wall Street devalues a company based on its performance rather than giving it credit for staying clean while some of its competitors skirt the limits of propriety.

Education Management Corporation

Education Management Corporation (EDMC) was founded in Pittsburgh in 1962. After several years of rather unremarkable activity as a professional development company in Pennsylvania, it purchased the Art Institute of Pittsburgh in 1970, making it the keystone of its expanding holdings in schools of art and design. Over the next twenty-five years, EDMC acquired nine more art schools and established one new school, marketing them as Art Institutes International. The art institutes, along with a New York City restaurant school and a small paralegal training school in Georgia, accounted for the holdings of EDMC when it went public in 1996 at $15 per share.

The company quickly purchased or opened eleven more art schools, in five years growing from 14,000 students in nine states to 28,000 students in sixteen states. In 2002 EDMC began expanding outside the art school realm with its purchase of Argosy Education Group, the largest for-profit provider of doctoral programs through its American Schools of Professional Psychology. Founded in 1975, Argosy enrolled sixty-three hundred students on eighteen campuses in nine states and Canada. In 2003 EDMC bought South University, a family-owned institution with four campuses in the southeastern United States, and the American Education Centers (AEC), an associate degree–granting institution with eighteen campuses in the Midwest. In addition, more schools of art and design were opened or acquired, bringing the Art Institutes system to thirty-one campuses in eighteen states and Canada. By the end of 2004, EDMC had combined the operations of Argosy into Argosy University and had renamed all the AEC campuses Brown Mackie College after a regionally accredited Kansas institution that was part of the AEC acquisition. All together, the company owns sixty-seven campuses in twenty-four states and Canada, serving 58,800 students in programs from diploma to doctorate.

EDMC uses several strategies in running the campuses it owns. The Argosy University system combines several formerly separate institutions operated by Argosy Education Group. Even though the original campuses had separate accreditations from three different accreditors, EDMC sought accreditation for Argosy from the North Central Association as a single institution. The Brown Mackie system, like Argosy University, comprises separate campuses acquired in the AEC purchase. Unlike Argosy, however, EDMC has not chosen to place them all under the same accreditation as a single institution; each retains its original accreditation and the Brown Mackie system operates as eight separately accredited institutions and associated branch campuses. This strategy is similar to that employed by the Art Institutes, where the acquired campuses retain local accreditation, although newly established locations are generally opened as accredited branches of existing schools. South University is operated as a stand-alone institution, with the former owner, John South, now employed by EDMC as the university's chancellor. Such diversity of operating strategies is unique among the public companies profiled here. Wall Street seems not to mind. The stock trades around $32 a share, and the company has the third-highest market value in the sector.

EVCI Career Colleges

EVCI is the youngest and, in terms of enrollment, the smallest public owner in the for-profit higher education sector. Founded in 1997 as Educational Video Conferencing Incorporated, the Yonkers, New York, company developed a proprietary network to deliver educational content from colleges to the employees of major corporations. EVCI was not an owner of any educational institution but rather had a few contracts for courses with local colleges and a half-dozen corporate clients. Even though the company was not profitable and had, as the prospectus for the initial public offering notes, an "unpredictable" cash flow, EVCI went public in 1999 at $12 a share. It promoted itself as a high-tech company and, though it remained unprofitable, saw its share prices rise to $40 in a booming stock market. In early 2000, this increase gave EVCI the capital to buy Interboro Institute, a New York City school with seven hundred students besieged by investigations of its participation in a state tuition program. So limited was EVCI's primary business that the small, struggling Interboro accounted for 87 percent of the company's revenues within three months of its purchase.

EVCI started looking for other for-profit schools to buy, completely shifting its focus from educational video to campus-based career education. In March 2000, however, the bottom dropped out of the stock market, and by the beginning of 2001, EVCI was struggling to avoid NASDAQ delisting for trading below $1 a share. Without capital, additional acquisitions were difficult, and the company made little progress after its first success with Interboro. In 2002, the company was renamed EVCI Career Colleges, and by 2003 the company posted its first profit, with Interboro providing its only source of income. EVCI has focused on expanding Interboro, opening four branch campuses around New York City and boosting enrollment to thirty-nine hundred in fall 2004. The strategy has been successful, and by the end of 2004, the company's stock was trading around $9 a share.

Distinctive among the for-profit companies profiled here, EVCI refuses to participate in student loan programs, specifically (it says) to avoid scrutiny or liability associated with student defaults. Although this stance limits the potential market for its programs (and perhaps even the tuition Interboro can charge), it does reduce risk for investors and may allow EVCI to serve a more disadvantaged student population. On the other hand, it removes one element of accountability that regulators have traditionally used to identify fraudulent practices. Whether it becomes a problem for EVCI or remains a source of comfort for the company's shareholders remains to be seen.

ITT Educational Services

ITT Educational Services is the parent company of ITT Technical Institute. Publicly owned since 1966, it has the longest history of continuous public ownership of any degree-granting for-profit institution of higher education in existence today. Founded in 1963 as Sams Technical Institute by an Indianapolis publisher of technical training manuals, Howard W. Sams and Company, the school quickly established four campuses in Indiana and Ohio. ITT Corporation purchased the publisher in 1966 and renamed the schools ITT Technical Institutes. ITT started a national expansion, opening new schools and acquiring others, and by 1970 had a system of twenty-two schools in the United States and five in Paris, France. Some of the less profitable schools were closed during the 1970s, leaving twenty-one schools in the system at the start of the 1980s. Another period of growth began as ITT acquired or opened more than a dozen schools through the mid-1980s.

In 1986, the company renamed all its schools ITT Technical Institutes and by the end of the decade developed Vision 2000, a plan for further geographic expansion as well as curricular expansion through the development of bachelor degree programs. But ITT was increasingly an anomaly in the for-profit educational world—a large system of schools run as a wholly owned subsidiary of a diversified corporate conglomerate. ITT's corporate parent decided that the stock market could give its schools needed visibility among investors, so in 1994, with fifty-four schools in twenty-five states and 22,000 students, 20 percent of the educational services division was spun off at a $10 per share initial public offering. The remaining 80 percent was held until 1999, when Starwood Hotels (which purchased ITT Corporation the year before) fully divested itself of all ownership in ITT Educational Services. Since then, ITT has been an independent pure-play education corporation.

ITT has continued to grow, increasing enrollment and adding locations every year. Its national presence and well-developed advertising campaign make it one of the highest-profile for-profit institutions in the country. By the end of 2004, ITT had more than 42,000 students enrolled in seventy-seven campuses in thirty states, with plans to offer joint programs in China with a Canadian for-profit school. The spate of investigations and scandals that hit the for-profit sector in 2004, however, directly affected ITT. The U.S. Department of Justice conducted a highly publicized raid on ten ITT campuses and the corporate headquarters, investigating allegations of falsification of attendance records, grades, and job placement statistics. SEC later opened its own investigation of the same matters, and a shareholder lawsuit predictably followed. It was not the first time that ITT has had these problems. In the mid-1990s, similar allegations came out of California in a lawsuit by former students. The company ultimately settled out of court, admitting no wrongdoing. This time with a federal investigation, grand jury subpoenas, and regulatory inquiries, the company faced more intense scrutiny. Still, ITT stock has rebounded from its scandal-driven mid-2004 decline and at the beginning of 2005 was trading around $50 a share.

Kaplan Higher Education

As a wholly owned subsidiary of the Washington Post Company, Kaplan Higher Education reflects more of the corporate organizational patterns of the 1960s and 1970s than those of today. Kaplan got its start as a training and testing center in the 1940s. The Washington Post Company acquired it in 1984, though it was more than a decade before Kaplan made its first foray into postsecondary education. In 1998, Kaplan began a small distance learning operation through two new entities: Concorde University School of Law and the College for Professional Studies. The big move came in 2000, however, when the Washington Post Company acquired its first Title IV–eligible schools through the purchase of Quest Education, forming the basis of its current Kaplan Higher Education division. Quest was founded in 1988 as Educational Medical, Inc. (EMI), with the purchase of five health services schools in California and Arizona. Over the next eight years, EMI slowly expanded into schools of business and fashion. At its $10 a share initial public offering in 1996, EMI owned fourteen schools in six states with an enrollment of forty-three hundred students. The company began to expand at a faster clip through acquisitions and in 1998, as it outgrew its medical heritage, was christened Quest Education. Quest stock never really caught on with investors, however, and trading remained around the $10 initial public offering price for the $115 million company. On its acquisition in 2000, the Washington Post Company paid a premium price of $18.35 a share for Quest's thirty-four schools and 12,800 students.

The Quest acquisition has proved to be quite valuable for the Washington Post Company. Called Kaplan Higher Education since 2002, the division now posts well over $400 million in annual revenues and is responsible for 45,000 students in seventy institutions across sixteen states as well as other locations in the United Kingdom and Asia. In terms of revenue, Kaplan is about the same size as ITT and Laureate, and only CEC owns more separate degree-granting institutions. Kaplan Higher Education accounts for 20 percent of the Washington Post Company's total revenue—second only to its newspaper business—and has been the company's fastest-growing division since the Quest acquisition in 2000. The higher education holdings of the Washington Post Company may in fact be significant enough to affect the parent company's stock prices. During summer 2004, when all the for-profit education companies saw their stock fall, the Washington Post Company's shares dropped 11 percent—a decline of more than $100 a share from its 2004 high. Even though no scandals or investigations have been reported at Kaplan schools, some analysts saw guilt by association as investors begin to notice the growing influence of for-profit higher education on the newspaper company's bottom line (Knight, 2004). Kaplan remains the only major owner of degree-granting institutions of higher education controlled by a diversified corporation, a resister in the era of the pure-play education company.

Laureate Education
Laureate originated in 1979 as a testing and tutoring company called Sylvan Learning Centers. Founded in Portland, Oregon, the company quickly expanded and had established franchises across the country when it was purchased by competitor KinderCare Learning Centers in 1985. KinderCare did little to support Sylvan and ultimately sold the learning centers division in 1991 to two young entrepreneurs as the company headed for bankruptcy.

Douglas Becker and Christopher Hoehn-Saric were both in their twenties and already millionaires when they purchased Sylvan for the bargain price of $8 million. They renamed the company Sylvan Learning Systems and took the company public in 1993 at an initial price of $11 a share. In the mid-1990s, the company began looking for opportunities to expand outside their core business of providing remedial education and testing services to school-age children. Sylvan acquired the Wall Street Institute, an English language instruction school with locations in Europe and Latin America to complement its growing international presence with learning centers. Domestically, the company made a big play to purchase NEC in 1997, ultimately losing out to Harcourt General, and the following year, Sylvan bought Canter, a teacher education company that provided contract degree programs to private colleges and universities in the United States. The company expanded into distance education in 1996 with the cofounding with MCI Corporation of the Caliber Learning Network.

Still, it was not until 1999 that Sylvan acquired its first degree-granting institution: Universidad Europea de Madrid. The Spanish university offered a full range of degrees, associate through doctorate, and became the foundation for a global network of for-profit institutions of higher education now called Laureate International Universities. Meanwhile, domestically, Sylvan focused on distance education, initially through its stake in Caliber and then, as that liaison proved unsuccessful, through the purchase of Walden University in 2001 and National Technical University (NTU) in 2002. In 2003 Sylvan decided to sell its original learning center business and focus on the higher education market. The following year, it adopted the name Laureate Education to emphasize its new identity in degree-granting postsecondary education.

Laureate is the dominant U.S.-based corporation in international for-profit higher education, owning seventeen university systems with forty-one campuses in eleven countries. Including distance learning opportunities available through Walden and NTU, Laureate serves 155,000 students, making it second in enrollment only to the Apollo Group. The company is distinctive in several ways. First, it is the only U.S. corporation in the higher education sector with the majority of its operations overseas. Four-fifths of its revenue and 85 percent of its enrollment come from its international universities division. Second, it is the only company with a growth strategy focused on the development and acquisition of degree-granting institutions, and it is the only one in which every institution it owns offers degree programs. It sold all of its learning centers and the nondegree Wall Street Institute when shifting to postsecondary education in 2003. Finally, it is the only company with no campus-based operations in the United States (though in 2004 it established a joint degree program with Kendall College in Illinois and has the option to purchase the not-for-profit culinary school in the future). To be eligible for Title IV funding, Walden and NTU participate in the U.S. Department of Education's distance education demonstration program.[10] Perhaps because it is such an unusual company in the sector and draws limited revenue from Title IV programs, it was the least affected of any for-profit education company during the scandal-driven stock declines in 2004. By the end of the year, Laureate stock was trading at an all-time high of $44 a share and had outperformed all other companies in the sector.

Strayer Education

Strayer has the longest history of any public corporation in the higher education sector. Founded more than one hundred years ago as Strayer Business College, the company has its roots in a shorthand method that was developed by Dr. S. Irving Strayer in 1890. Strayer opened his first school in Baltimore in 1892 and, with typewriter distributor Thomas Donoho as half-owner, opened branch campuses in Washington, D.C., and Philadelphia in 1904. Donoho bought out Strayer in 1910, and his family owned the school for the next seventy years. A new owner in 1980 guided the institution through an initial Middle States Association accreditation in 1981 and added the first new campus since 1904 by expanding into Virginia. In 1989, Ron Bailey, a former instructor at Strayer, bought the company for $5 million, closed the original Baltimore campus, and began expanding in the Washington, D.C., area. When the company went public in 1996, it operated eight campuses and served seventy-five hundred students. The initial offering price of $10 a share soon proved to be a bargain, as nine months later the company made a second offering at $21.75 a share.

The capital raised in these offerings allowed the company to accelerate its growth. It was renamed Strayer University in 1998 and opened six new campuses in four years, nearly doubling enrollment and expanding degree programs. In 2000 Bailey retired and new leadership took over. Backed by an infusion of venture capital, Strayer began expanding outside of the Washington, D.C., area, opening campuses in Tennessee, Pennsylvania, Georgia, and North Carolina, and South Carolina. By the end of 2004, Strayer had thirty campuses in seven states and Washington, D.C., and served approximately 23,000 students.

Strayer's expansion continues apace, with new campuses planned for Florida in 2005. Overall enrollment, however, remains comparatively low. Nearly half the students study through Strayer's online campus, making the average enrollment per physical location fewer than 500 students. The company's growth strategy explains some of this anomaly. Rather than building the Strayer University system by acquiring other for-profit institutions (along with their students), the company has moved into markets and established new schools under the Strayer University name. It also has a regional strategy for expansion, concentrating on the mid-Atlantic and southeastern United States, rather than jumping immediately to large markets across the country. Even though it is the oldest company in terms of its corporate heritage, Strayer University is the newest addition to the ranks of national shareholder universities; only since 2001 has it developed a significant multistate presence. The explosive growth since then, however, has been attractive to investors, with stock trading at higher than $100 a share—giving Strayer the highest stock price in current dollars (with the exception of the Washington Post Company, which trades at more than $900 per share)—and offering dividends nearly every quarter since its 1996 initial public offering.

Universal Technical Institute
A public company since 2003, Universal Technical Institute (UTI) is the newest shareholder owner of degree-granting for-profit higher education. Founded in 1965 as a Phoenix automotive mechanics school, the company has not strayed far from its roots. From the single Phoenix location, UTI opened campuses in Houston and Chicago in the 1980s and established a

continuing education program to retrain technicians for major automobile manufacturers. The company was purchased by venture capitalists in 1998 and combined with the Clinton Technical Institute, a company that operated two schools of motorcycle and marine maintenance. The following year, UTI developed a NASCAR-sponsored technical school, and by the time of the public offering in 2003, UTI was offering a focused technical curriculum through these three division at seven campuses in six states and twenty-two additional centers sponsored by manufacturers. A new campus was opened in 2004, serving a total enrollment of 13,000 students in diploma and certificate programs as well as an associate in occupational studies. Clearly different from the other shareholder owners in terms of the narrow and technical focus of its curriculum, UTI is the largest provider of training in the automotive and marine mechanics field in the United States. As such, it represents a prestigious institution in its field and, like most of the other public companies, has been popular with investors. Its initial offering price of $20.50 rose to more than $35 a share by the end of 2004. Rarely mentioned in discussions of the for-profit higher education sector, it nonetheless represents an important segment in the sector and another dimension of the Wall Street era.

Implications of the Wall Street Era

Beginning in the late 1990s, the development of publicly owned for-profit companies was recognized as a growing trend (see, for example, Kelly, 2001; Marchese, 1998; Ortmann, 2001; Ruch, 2001; Strosnider, 1998). Initial reports generally focused on the competitive threat posed by these "new providers" on the one hand and the attractiveness of their academic model to the market on the other. Proponents of the sector emphasized their managerial and academic efficiency with the potential to transform the higher education industry, while critics reminded readers of the enormous government subsidies supporting this profit-making enterprise and the history of fraud in the sector that demanded close regulatory attention. Questions have been raised about the lobbying influence of for-profit corporations on federal policymaking (Pusser and Wolcott, 2003) and their decisions to use and manipulate accreditation status as part of a business plan (Kinser, 2005d).

Little agreement has been reached on these points, and the implications of the trend toward greater Wall Street control over degree-granting for-profit higher education is not clear. Three hypotheses are offered here.

First, the growth of public corporate ownership has reduced the connection to the local community formerly maintained by the independent proprietary school. The small for-profit institutions of earlier eras were essentially local institutions, founded to serve particular needs and often named after the proprietor with specific ties to the community. The new corporate-owned institutions are franchise-like in their operation, either establishing branch campuses designed to extend the brand or purchasing local campuses and converting them to fit into an expansive corporate bureaucracy. In the same way that the distinctiveness of the independent bookstore and hardware store is lost to the superstore sameness of Barnes & Noble and the Home Depot, national shareholder institutions like DeVry, ITT, Strayer, and the University of Phoenix replace idiosyncratic owner-operators of the for-profit sector with an impersonal corporate face and mass-market techniques.

Second, corporate-owned institutions are increasingly positioned as narrow competitors to traditional higher education in cash-cow fields rather than niche providers for students ill served by conventional institutions. In a form of for-profit mission creep, shareholder institutions have tended to develop new programs in high-demand fields regardless of their original mission and focus. Degrees in business and allied health fields are paired with paralegal programs and technical trades. Non-degree-granting institutions are combined into a system with a focus on awarding degrees. Academic models originally designed for career-changing adults are applied to targeted career training for recent high school graduates. The scope of the education offered is narrow—there are no liberal arts graduates in the for-profit sector—but it more directly competes with the academic programs and student markets of traditional institutions. Especially as the nonprofit educational world becomes more market oriented, the corporate-owned for-profit institutions have the capital and confidence necessary to take on their much larger rivals.

Third, corporate owners have destabilized the sector by establishing a culture of growth that demands short-term returns to finance continued expansion.[11] Sperling (2000) is quite clear in asserting that Wall Street would be interested in a University of Phoenix public offering only if it could generate double-digit growth. Ortmann (2001) validates this perspective in his assessment of the market evaluation of the for-profit sector. Growth is achieved through expanding existing operations or acquiring additional institutions, and public corporations have used these strategies to develop some of the largest systems of higher education in the United States. Moreover, nearly all the corporate owners profiled here have a strategy of developing new programs and curricula that can be rolled out to other locations and a strategy that relies on part-time contract faculty. Although the local ownership of earlier eras could be satisfied with a few hundred students studying a fairly stable curriculum, the corporate owners must see quarterly "same-store" growth achieved through expanding student markets. The turmoil encouraged by such growth creates a different environment for the for-profit sector, with challenges for management as well as academic personnel seeking to adjust to the pressures associated with Wall Street's bottom-line evaluations.

These three hypotheses are just that; they are not statements of fact. Community connections, competitive forces, and sector stability may not be much different from the past. Little is known about the impact of different ownership models on for-profit institutional practice. But when 160-year-old Duff's Business College is acquired by ten-year-old Corinthian Colleges after its former owner, Phillips Colleges, collapses in scandal, one can suspect that the transitions involved in those ownership changes were not particularly smooth. When the American Institute of Commerce changes its name twice in three years—to reflect the preferences of its new corporate owners—it is hard not to think that the Iowa community that supported the institution since 1937 must be taking a back seat. And when South University receives permission to offer the Doctor of Pharmacy degree shortly after its purchase by EDMC, the curricular expansion is notable for an institution that just a few years earlier was a small family-owned business college in Savannah, Georgia. Certainly the beginnings of the Wall Street era have brought the for-profit sector to the attention of the larger higher education community. The changes that it has wrought on the sector itself are only now becoming evident. As the shift continues toward a shareholder-owned model, internecine battles may become more evident and their impact more clear.

Measure of Success: Students in the For-Profit Sector

T HE ORGANIZATION OF FOR-PROFIT HIGHER EDUCATION reflects the sector's institutional diversity. Students' participation, on the other hand, suggests a different sort of diversity: Who attends these schools? Why do they enroll? What experiences do they have in and out of class? Fundamentally important to the existence of for-profit higher education, the student is the target audience for institutional expansion and primary arbiter of the sector's ultimate success. From the perspective of traditional not-for-profit private and public higher education, the competition posed by the for-profit sector lies in its ability to attract students to its programs. The growing number of students drawn to degree-granting for-profits in the Wall Street era, in fact, is one of the most obvious examples of the transformation of the sector.

Much is known about the demographics of students attending for-profit schools; less is understood about their reasons for enrolling and their experiences in these institutions and once they leave. Because of its impact on public policy, most of the currently available information relates to students' participation in Title IV programs and those enrolled in degree-granting for-profit institutions. It is surprising that there are so few comprehensive studies of students at for-profit institutions. Moreover, given that current research on traditional college students increasingly uses qualitative methodology (Pascarella and Terenzini, 2005), it is noteworthy that the quantitative perspective so heavily dominates when looking at students in the for-profit sector.

Historical Perspectives

The students who attend for-profit institutions of higher education have been the subject of study since the U.S. Office of Education began surveying these institutions in 1870. Until roughly World War II, data were primarily limited to enrollment numbers and basic demographic information, much of which is incomplete (Bolino, 1973; Miller and Hamilton, 1964). Even so, some interesting trends can be identified that relate to aspects of students' participation in the for-profit sector today. Two items are of particular note. First, enrollment growth and decline are related to government legislation and regulation. Absent any state involvement in their business of career and vocational education, for-profit schools were initially free to grow as large as the free market would allow. The Morrill Land Grant Acts of 1862 and 1890, however, affected the way the public sector viewed nonacademic education, and the place of vocationalism in the educational system became an important topic around the turn of the twentieth century (Grubb and Lazerson, 2004; Venn, 1964). Enrollments declined in the for-profit sector and then rose again as public institutions initially embraced career education only to pull back as the academic and cultural purposes of education were reasserted. The 1917 Smith-Hughes Act signaled a substantial and permanent shift toward public support of vocational education, and almost immediately student enrollment moved to the newly subsidized institutions. Declining enrollments continued for twenty years until for-profit institutions were included as part of the mix of schools authorized to assist the government in meeting the training demands of World War II; after the war, the GI bill funded a boom in proprietary school enrollments (Petrello, 1987). Similar fluctuations in for-profit sector enrollment are visible in the 1970s and 1990s, likely in response to regulations motivated by scandals in federal aid programs.

The second element of these historical enrollment figures is that the for-profit sector has often provided a point of access for students who are underrepresented or denied participation in the traditional higher education sectors. It is particularly evident with respect to the enrollment of women. At the turn of the century, James (1900) accurately noted that women had been significant beneficiaries of nineteenth-century for-profit business schools. Coeducation became common among business schools after the development of the type-writer in 1876 opened up office work to women (Bolino, 1973). Although men greatly outnumbered women in for-profit institutions through 1890, much of the enrollment growth during this period was the result of increasing numbers of women attracted to for-profit business schools. By 1910, females were enrolling at similar levels as males, and by the end of that decade (likely augmented by World War I declines in the available male population), women outnumbered men (Bolino, 1973). Gender parity in the for-profit sector, then, occurred decades before men and women enjoyed similar levels of access in the not-for-profit private and public sectors. Today, this issue of access is displayed in the relatively higher proportional enrollment of low-income and minority students in the for-profit sector than in traditional institutions of higher education (Phipps, Harrison, and Merisotis, 1999).

Other than general enrollment surveys, the first real research on students attending for-profit higher education began after World War II, mostly in response to veterans' taking advantage of the GI bill (Petrello, 1987). These studies were episodic and rarely rose beyond the simple conclusion that veterans would choose for-profit institutions when given the choice. Federal funding through the GI bill led to the establishment of formal accreditation procedures and with them a drive to understand the quality of services the for-profit sector provides to students. Studies conducted of the membership of the United Business Schools Association in the late 1950s and early 1960s represent the first concerted effort to characterize (among other things) those who attend proprietary institutions, and the National Business Teachers Association published several volumes during the same period providing an overview of ongoing research about student outcomes by faculty in the for-profit sector (Miller and Hamilton, 1964). Because this initial research was conducted by advocates of the sector, however, it was not intended to present a critical perspective and provides little empirical evidence to support claims of successful educational performance.

Research on students by traditional academics began during the early 1960s, likewise influenced by the availability of federal money to support students at for-profit institutions. Miller and Hamilton (1964) note that "the State University of Iowa" established a research program on private business education in 1962 and suggest enrollment trends and student dropouts as topics that should be covered. This reference is likely to the University of Iowa's specialty-oriented student research program organized by Kenneth B. Hoyt, which surveyed a sample of students at approximately fifty private trade schools between 1963 and 1966 to provide better information to high school guidance counselors about noncollegiate educational options available to career-oriented students (Hoyt, 1965). Original reports that describe the findings of this investigation are difficult to find. The first book-length investigation by independent researchers was Clark and Sloan's *Classrooms on Main Street* (1966), though they concentrate more on the organization and regulation of the industry than on the students who attend for-profit institutions.

It is not until Belitsky (1969) published *Private Vocational Schools and Their Students* in 1969 that an extensive empirical study of students attending for-profit institutions appears in the literature. Belitsky concludes that for-profit institutions have an important role to play in serving disadvantaged students and provides evidence to support the expansion of federal loan programs. Intriguing nuggets of information about students attending for-profit institutions in the 1960s still seem relevant today. For example, two-thirds of the schools enroll "overeducated" students, and in one sample of six hundred technical students, 22 percent had previously attended a traditional college or university. In a third of the institutions studied, the majority of students live more than fifty miles from campus, and two-thirds have matriculated foreign students. Displaying great prescience toward the future role of government-backed loans across higher education, for-profit students in the 1960s not only reported borrowing substantial amounts of money but also indicated they were willing to borrow more (Belitsky, 1969), in essence foreshadowing the 1972 reauthorization of the Higher Education Act that opened up federally guaranteed borrowing privileges to students in the for-profit sector.

The new availability of student loans after 1972 created a new interest in the for-profit sector (see Erwin, 1975), though Trivett (1974) notes in his review of the literature that information on student attendance patterns and outcomes is still lacking. He points out that the value of the education provided by for-profit institutions ought to be easily measured but that so little is known about the sector that no strong conclusions can be reached. Even the typical proprietary school student remained relatively unknown, with only general hypotheses suggesting that for-profit students probably:

- Were younger than twenty-five.
- Selected proprietary school because it offered a short course to a job.
- Were well-enough educated to attend other types of schools if desired.
- Borrowed money directly or through deferred payment in order to attend.
- Will find a training-related job. [Trivett, 1974, p. 31]

Some of the tentative nature of Trivett's review (1974) was corrected by the research of William Hyde (1976) and Wellford Wilms (1974) and a study conducted by the American Institutes for Research (Jung, Campbell, and Wolman, 1976). All focused on the effectiveness of for-profit institutions compared with public sector vocational training institutions. Depending on one's perspective, the two types of schools are equally effective (Jung, Campbell, and Wolman, 1976) or ineffective (Wilms, 1974) in meeting students' needs. Wilms (1974), however, goes into some detail about differences between students who attend for-profit versus public institutions, concluding that proprietary students tend to have their educational aspirations suppressed, even as they were more likely to graduate. Wilms attributes this difference to a "cooling out" function in the proprietary sector, suggesting that although the for-profit sector enrolls a greater proportion of lower-socioeconomic-status individuals, it does little to challenge existing educational inequalities in society.

For more than a decade after these studies, research on students in the for-profit sector did not make much progress. The Belitsky study (1969) remained the most comprehensive analysis, and a review of the literature conducted in the late 1980s notes that "the few studies that have been conducted since 1980 . . . confirm earlier findings" (Lee and Merisotis, 1990, p. 28). To summarize, the consensus at the beginning of the Wall Street era was that students in for-profit institutions are more likely to be minorities from low-income backgrounds with lower tested abilities and weaker academic backgrounds than students in not-for-profit private and public institutions. They are also older on average than other college students and less likely to depend on their parents for financial support. They are, in general, most similar to community college students. Some hints of a coming transformation, however, were in evidence. Apling (1993) notes that for-profit schools may be enrolling younger students than earlier studies had indicated. Cheng and Levin (1995) argue that the student populations of for-profit schools and community colleges have been changing, and their analysis suggests that few distinctions remain between the two sectors' students. Grubb (1993) suggests that the emphasis on low-income and minority students' attending for-profit institutions is overstated and can be explained by the urban location of most of these schools. Combined, these factors point to a for-profit sector that, for traditional colleges and universities, was beginning to represent a source of competition for student enrollments.

National Datasets

The real significance of studies since the late 1980s, though, was in their use of new national datasets from the U.S. Department of Education. Longitudinal surveys sponsored by NCES began to bear fruit during this period, and students at for-profit institutions could for the first time be readily compared with those attending not-for-profit private and public institutions. The National Longitudinal Study of the High School Class of 1972 (NLS 72) and the High School and Beyond Survey of the Class of 1980 (HSB 80) first provided solid data on the attendance patterns of high schools students, while the National Postsecondary Student Aid Study (NPSAS) began in 1986 to provide significant details about students' family background, financial circumstances, and demographic characteristics. A fourth survey, the Beginning Postsecondary Students Longitudinal Study (BPS), follows cohorts of students identified in NPSAS through their college careers and provides information on their undergraduate experiences and transitions into the workforce. Finally, enrollment figures from the Higher Education General Information Survey (HEGIS) became readily available in the 1980s, and its successor survey, the Integrated Postsecondary Education Data System, has continued to provide these figures annually since 1986.[12] These surveys have been the nearly exclusive sources of information on students in the for-profit sector since 1990.

The key questions initially related to student loan defaults—who does not pay back a guaranteed loan and why. Apart from fraudulent activities on the part of some for-profits, the new national data established that it is generally not the institution but the student who is responsible for the default. Lee (1990) [cited in Lee and Merisotis, 1990] developed a risk score using NPSAS data that assigned low possibility for loan default to students from white, Asian, or high socioeconomic backgrounds, males, and those with no children. High risk was assigned to students from African American, Hispanic, or low socioeconomic backgrounds who were female, divorced, or widowed or had children. Students with more risk factors tended to default more often than those with fewer risk factors, and those students were more likely to attend non-degree-granting for-profit schools. Lee concluded that efforts to reduce loan defaults should not focus on the for-profit sector but on the students themselves. Others conducted similar analyses (Dynarski, 1994, for example), reaching the "obvious" conclusion: a program that encourages borrowing by high-risk individuals will see high rates of defaults.

Apart from the information regarding defaulters, a few additional details regarding the characteristics of students attending for-profit schools became clear. Approximately one-third are interested in earning degrees, for example, and substantial numbers indicate aspirations for graduate work (St. John, Starkey, Paulson, and Mbaduagha, 1995). More significant for understanding the transformation of the for-profit sector, however, are the demographic changes over time. In the 1970s, for example, women and minorities increased their proportional enrollment in the for-profit sector, as did those from low-income backgrounds and weaker academic abilities (Grubb, 1989). In the 1980s, students in for-profit institutions became moderately more nontraditional (Horn and Carroll, 1996), while in the 1990s, demographic and enrollment characteristics of students in less-than-four-year for-profit institutions were not much changed from the 1980s (Phipps, Harrison, and Merisotis, 1999). On the other hand, trends during the 1990s in four-year for-profit institutions suggest more of an ongoing transformation in the sector, with enrollments becoming substantially different from those in the two-year and nondegree for-profit institutions. Compared with students in less-than-four-year institutions, students at four-year institutions were more likely to be male, white, and from upper-income quartiles and were less likely to attend full time (Phipps, Harrison, and Merisotis, 1999).

Current Trends

The differences noted between students at four-year and less-than-four-year institutions (Phipps, Harrison, and Merisotis, 1999) documents an important shift in for-profit higher education: the development of a substantial degree-seeking student population in the for-profit sector. Although degree-granting for-profit institutions have existed since at least the 1950s, the number of students enrolled in these programs remained comparatively low. Only eight hundred students were enrolled in accredited "senior colleges" of business in 1964 (Petrello, 1987), representing just 1 percent of the total number of students in all accredited for-profit business schools. The numbers of students in degree programs seems to have been so small through the 1970s, in fact, that few authors even mention them. Beginning in 1976, however, NCES data identify a growing set of "proprietary institutions of higher education" that can serve as a proxy for for-profit degree-granting institutions through 1995. Students enrolled in these institutions remained a substantial minority during much of this time. Based on NCES data, total enrollment in the for-profit sector in 1980 was approximately 1.16 million students (Wilms, 1983), with 112,000 in proprietary institutions of higher education (National Center for Education Statistics, 2003a). Enrollment in these schools nearly doubled in the 1980s yet still represented less than 30 percent of the total population of for-profit students by the end of the decade (Horn, Khazzoom, and Carroll, 1993).

In the 1990s, the picture changed dramatically. Even though enrollments in for-profit institutions of higher education remained fairly flat in the early 1990s, declining numbers of students in noncollegiate institutions brought enrollments to nearly 40 percent of the total by 1995. An NCES tabulation of postsecondary institutions in 1996 showed the newly defined for-profit degree-granting sector accounted for slightly more than half of all enrollments, a proportion that increased to two-thirds by 1998, where it stayed for the rest of the decade (National Center for Education Statistics, 2003a). In the space of a decade, then, student enrollments in the for-profit sector essentially flip-flopped, shifting from nondegree to degree-granting institutions.

The enrollment shift to degree-granting institutions has come most significantly at four-year institutions. Between 1996 and 2001, enrollments at four-year degree-granting institutions increased by 190,000 students, representing 85 percent of the increase in enrollments at degree-granting institutions. Two-year degree-granting institutions increased by only 33,000 students during the same period, for the remaining 15 percent. This finding suggests not only changing educational levels but also a changing student population. Since 1980, for example, the ratio of men to women in degree-granting for-profit higher education has been roughly 50–50. Two-year institutions have seen little change in the proportion of women enrolled, with about 55 percent of the student body for the last twenty years. Men have historically enrolled in much greater proportions in four-year institutions—in 1980 nearly 70 percent of students in four-year for-profits were male—but that traditional dominance has been substantially modified. By 2001 the proportion of men enrolled in four-year institutions had declined to 53 percent. More women, therefore, are choosing a four-year institution, and 80 percent of the increase in for-profit female enrollments since 1996 has come at four-year degree-granting institutions.

Data for nondegree institutions are more difficult to tabulate consistently before 1996, though a substantial decline in enrollments in the nondegree for-profit sector is implied by the figures cited in a sequence of publications through the 1980s and early 1990s (Apling, 1993; Byce and Schmitt, 1992; Grubb, 1989; Jung, 1980; Lee and Merisotis, 1990; Wilms, 1983). Since 1996, NCES data (2003a) place the non-degree-granting institutional enrollment decline at 16 percent, or 47,000 students. During this period (1996–2001), the ratio of men to women in these institutions has shifted from 36:64 to 28:72 (National Center for Education Statistics, 2003a). In other words, nondegree for-profit institutions are becoming as a whole nearly single-sex schools, perhaps relating to changing curricula at these institutions.[13] The implications, though, are evident to calculations of gender diversity in the for-profit sector as a whole. Numerically, female enrollment is concentrated in nondegree institutions—almost 40 percent of the total female population—even as nearly all of the increasing number of women in the for-profit sector matriculate at four-year schools.

Additional information tracking other demographic characteristics of students in the for-profit sector is available in the raw NPSAS and IPEDS data files but has not been published. Based on the analyses of Phipps, Harrison, and Merisotis (1999) of data from the mid-1990s, however, it is likely that differences continue. Some evidence of these differences comes from a report (Center for Policy Analysis, 2004) that notes the decline in low-income students at for-profit, less-than-four-year institutions between 1989 and 1999. This change may be the result of the growing proportion of students at for-profit degree-granting institutions—students who are less likely to be from low-income backgrounds—compared with the real enrollment decline at nondegree schools. Other data suggest that four-year for-profits are less likely to serve large minority populations than are two-year institutions (National Center for Education Statistics, 2003a, Table 208). Finally, Chung (2004) notes the heterogeneity of the for-profit student population and suggests three statistically distinct student populations corresponding to the nondegree, two-year, and four-year institutional levels reported in NPSAS data. The increase in enrollments at four-year institutions, combined with the decreases seen in nondegree institutions, certainly has an effect on the changing student demographics of the sector as a whole. It is likely, then, that the for-profit sector in the Wall Street era is serving proportionally fewer minorities, low-income students, younger students, and part-time students than it was in earlier eras because of different enrollment rates by degree level.

Student Outcomes

With so many critiques of the for-profit sector focused on the quality of the education provided to its students and the public policy rationale for providing student aid to the for-profit sector, it is perhaps surprising that so little data are available on student outcomes. Several authors tackled this question in the 1970s and 1980s (Jung, Campbell, and Wolman, 1976; Wilms and Hansell, 1983), generally concluding that the for-profit school provided weaker economic returns to graduates than did public sector institutions. A more recent analysis also finds that proprietary schools do not do a particularly good job of increasing the earnings of their graduates (Grubb, 1993). This research, however, tracks students who graduated from for-profit institutions in a regulatory environment and labor market that had changed substantially by the 1990s and continues to be in flux today. It is not clear whether the rather consistent findings of the previous three decades regarding the relatively weaker economic benefits of a for-profit education would hold under current conditions. The development in the Wall Street era of much larger institutions with national reputations and the granting of degrees that seem quite similar to those offered in the not-for-profit private and public sectors may have shifted the calculus for some students. Moreover, the different economic circumstances of a technology- and information-driven economy may reward short-term attendance and nondegree credentials more now than in the past (Adelman, 2000). Whether attending a for-profit institution makes a difference in this respect is not known.[14]

Simple attendance, of course, is not really the point. Whether students actually complete a degree or credential at a for-profit institution certainly affects their ability to gain the benefit of time spent. In the 1970s, approximately 40 percent of students at for-profit institutions left without earning a credential, and the proportion of dropouts was essentially the same for students beginning in 1972 and 1980 (Grubb, 1989). Interestingly, BPS data from students beginning in 1995 at two-year for-profit institutions show the same proportion—40 percent—of noncompleters by 2001 (National Center for Education Statistics, 2004b). Both historically and contemporarily, for-profit institutions show better graduation rates than their public sector competitors at the two-year level. Community colleges report a 42 percent rate for noncompleters who began in 1980 and a 46 percent rate for those who began in 1995 (Grubb, 1989; National Center for Education Statistics, 2004b). On the other hand, the BPS data suggest that two-year for-profit institutions do not facilitate transfer to four-year institutions. Only 2 percent of students who initially enrolled in two-year for-profits had earned a bachelor's degree by 2001, compared with 12 percent in not-for-profit two-year institutions and 10 percent in community colleges. Moreover, two-year for-profits do not seem to be good choices for students who are long-term persisters. Just 4 percent of the students who began in these institutions were still enrolled after six years, compared with 8 percent in not-for-profit two-year institutions and 17 percent in community colleges (National Center for Education Statistics, 2004b).

Although comparable information is not available for four-year institutions before 1995, the data for students beginning in that year show that 36 percent of students in for-profit institutions were no longer enrolled in 2001 and had not earned any credential—compared with 22 percent noncompleters in the public sector and 17 percent among private not-for-profit institutions at the four-year level (National Center for Education Statistics, 2004b). Not only do fewer students complete a credential, fewer actually earn a bachelor's degree. Just 20 percent of the for-profit students had earned a bachelor's degree by 2001, compared with 53 percent of the public institutions and 69 percent of the private, for-profit institutions. Students attending four-year for-profit institutions were quite likely to leave with just a certificate (18 percent) or an associate degree (15 percent). These outcomes were uncommon—fewer than 5 percent of students—outside the for-profit sector.

Taken together, these data suggest that for-profit institutions are rather successful at helping students earn an associate degree or a certificate but are less useful if the student wishes to earn a bachelor's degree. This statement does not, of course, take students' intentions into consideration (nor does it consider structural barriers, such as credit transfer limitations based on accreditation status). Perhaps students who enroll in the for-profit sector are interested in earning a credential quickly and the shorter certificates and associate degrees better meet their needs (see Bailey, Badway, and Gumport, 2003; Kelly, 2001; and Ruch, 2001, for some anecdotal support), though no comprehensive survey of students' intentions has been completed. The lower graduation rates at four-year institutions could also be an effect of the same student perspective. If for-profit students have a strong desire to finish quickly, they may be discouraged by the time it takes to earn a bachelor's degree.[15] Finally, these data track only the outcomes for first-time postsecondary students who began their studies in one sector versus another. They do not consider the impact of transfers across sectors. It is possible that the for-profit sector is much more successful in helping returning students or students transferring from traditional institutions. Nevertheless, the academic outcomes for students are substantially different if they initially attend a for-profit institution rather than institutions in the not-for-profit private and public sectors.

Apart from academic and economic outcomes, many in traditional higher education are concerned with the social, affective, or developmental benefits of going to college. The concern does not seem to extend to research on for-profit higher education. The rare exception is Persell and Wenglinsky's analysis (2004) of civic engagement by students who attend for-profit institutions. Using questions in the BPS regarding political participation and civic-mindedness, they developed a measure of civic engagement for community college and proprietary school students who began college in 1990. Controlling for various demographic and background variables, Persell and Wenglinsky (2004) found that students in the for-profit sector are less likely to vote, less likely to participate in other political activities, and less likely to become involved in their communities than are students in community colleges. They concluded that for-profit higher education actually reduces the societal benefits of attending college, which (they argue) questions the rationale for using public money to support students attending these institutions.

Although it is tempting simply to connect the institutional pursuit of profit to the decline of civic responsibility in students, the mechanism for such a link deserves some scrutiny. Perhaps by directing students to focus on job preparation, broader purposes of education are actually devalued. Alternatively, as mentioned in the discussion of shareholder owners, it could be evidence that geographically distant corporate owners have less of a connection to the local community and thus less understanding of how to inspire community engagement in their students. Although the former explanation would apply to all for-profits equally, the latter rationale would imply different effects, depending on whether the student attended, for example, a neighborhood enterprise institute or a national shareholder university.

Student Motivation, Experiences, and Campus Life

Apart from their intriguing findings, Persell and Wenglinsky (2004) demonstrate that U.S. Department of Education surveys contain much unexplored data on students in the for-profit sector beyond the demographics of the student population. But these datasets offer little detail on students' motivations to attend for-profit institutions or their experiences once enrolled. Unfortunately, very few other sources of information are available. The Cooperative Institutional Research Program (CIRP) Freshman Survey has included for-profit institutions in its sample since it began in 1966 (Cooperative Institutional Research Program, 2004), but published summaries have not generally reported findings from the sector. Ruch (2001) notes that DeVry regularly participates in the Noel-Levitz Student Satisfaction Inventory. Using these data, he finds that students at this institution rate their campus climate as highly as do students at "traditional" campuses and actually rate campus life higher (p. 133). As Ruch's access to this information is presumably through his employment as a DeVry administrator, no additional analyses are available. The CIRP or the Noel-Levitz surveys could provide additional information about students at participating institutions if those data were accessible for further analyses.

Unlike studies of students in the not-for-profit private and public sectors, almost no smaller-scale surveys exist of students in for-profit higher education. Qualitative studies that report for-profit students' perspectives are likewise rare. As part of a larger study of the for-profit sector, for example, the Education Commission of the States conducted interviews with students and administrators on thirteen campuses (Kelly, 2001). Data from these interviews suggest that students attend for-profit institutions because of better student services, more direct application to their career goals, and dissatisfaction with experiences at traditional institutions. The reasons given are similar to those reported by Kincaid and Podesta (cited in Trivett, 1974) and Friedlander (1980) from interviews conducted in the 1960s and 1970s. In another study, Deil-Amen and Rosenbaum (2003) interviewed students and administrators at a set of for-profit institutions in the Midwest and surveyed more than forty-three hundred additional students in community colleges and for-profit institutions. Their findings suggest that students at for-profit institutions generally have better experiences with student services than those in community colleges and are better able to complete their degree in a timely manner with a minimum of bureaucratic hassles. Given the scant research in this area, however, the experiences and expectations of students in for-profit higher education are simply not well understood.

At least some for-profit institutions with college-sponsored residential facilities, athletics, student clubs, and other elements of a traditional student life program exist, however (Bailey, Badway, and Gumport, 2003; Kelly, 2001; Kinser, 2005d). Academic or career-specific student groups seem quite common, with other extracurricular activities occasionally available at degree-granting institutions. For most for-profit institutions, however, student services are directed toward the academic support of students rather than social activities (Kinser, 2005c). Contrasting this finding with the perspectives of student affairs at traditional institutions, Kinser (2005c) summarizes five principles of student affairs in the for-profit sector. First, student affairs is a core institutional function in the for-profit sector directed toward serving and supporting students as customers. Second, helping a student matriculate, stay enrolled, and graduate is the primary focus of student affairs in for-profit higher education. Third, for-profit student affairs understands the personal and academic issues faced by a nontraditional student body and designs services with that population in mind. Fourth, student affairs at for-profit institutions is oriented toward creating an out-of-class environment that is conducive to learning. And fifth, convenience in the for-profit sector is key, as student affairs follows the student and makes accessing services and support as simple and direct as possible.

Remaining Questions

Information on the current status of students in the for-profit sector remains sketchy. In addition to the obvious lack of data on students' experiences in for-profit higher education, other areas continue to be largely unexplored. Unlike the not-for-profit private and public sectors, remarkably little research is available on students coming from a student affairs perspective. The broad literature on student development theory has not touched the for-profit sector; the cognitive or social-psychological impact of a for-profit education on students is unknown. It is also not clear who is responsible for student services in the for-profit sector and the extent to which these individuals have formal training in student affairs. Further questions revolve around whether for-profit institutional rhetoric regarding a student-centered education is matched by the reality of the student services actually offered. Finally, the profit motive may convert student affairs into customer service. Whether this situation is the for-profit future of student affairs (Kinser, 2005c) remains to be seen.

The Academic Mission:
Teaching and Learning
in the For-Profit Sector

FROM AN ORGANIZATIONAL PERSPECTIVE, the for-profit sector has always included a range of ownership models, and enrollment has continued on a fairly steady trajectory since World War II. The transformation of the for-profit sector in the Wall Street era, however, is exemplified in its changing academic mission. Once rare, the degree-granting for-profit institution is now ascendant, from the associate to the doctoral level (Kelly, 2001). Along with growth in terms of students and facilities, the curriculum too has expanded. The focus in earlier eras on entry-level business, trade, and technical skills has developed in the Wall Street era to include a range of professional disciplines such as education, psychology, and law. But although the idea of a singular for-profit academic model is a myth, the fundamental vocational character of the for-profit sector remains, and even degree-granting institutions still award a substantial number of nondegree certificates (Bailey, Badway, and Gumport, 2003). At its core, the mission of for-profit higher education is to teach students. The previous chapter discussed the students. This chapter is about what is taught in the for-profit sector and who teaches it.

Curriculum

For-profit institutions have historically offered curricula that are narrowly directed toward a specific career. Initially that career was business. Herrick's early account (1904) describes the curriculum at Metropolitan

Business College in Chicago as typical of the time:

A commercial or business program that includes bookkeeping, business math, correspondence, law, writing, and basic calculation;

An amanuensis program that includes shorthand, typewriting, letter writing, penmanship, spelling, and grammar; and

An advanced (second-year) business program that includes commercial geography, higher accounting, political economy, advertising, civil government, parliamentary law, commerce and finance, and modern languages (Herrick, 1904, pp. 304–305).

Beginning in the late nineteenth century, other types of schools were founded that offered training for different careers. For-profit barber schools, art schools, trade schools, and flight schools all existed alongside business schools before World War II, and by the 1960s, there were hundreds of programs at thousands of schools ranged from accounting to wig making (Clark and Sloan, 1966). In the 1970s with the advent of more expansive data collecting by NCES, nine curricular categories for the for-profit sector were established, including technical fields, trades, business, cosmetology, flight, art and design, and allied health (Jung, 1980). By the 1990s, the number of primary fields had been reduced to six: business, personal services (which includes cosmetology), health, technology, trades, and transportation (which includes flight training) (Apling, 1993). The number of flight schools had declined, while the number of cosmetology and business schools had increased. These basic curricular areas remain descriptive of the scope of the for-profit sector through the 1990s.

Even with expansion during the Wall Street era, the business curriculum has continued as the mainstay of the for-profit sector. In the 1970s and 1980s, approximately 45 percent of all students in for-profit higher education were enrolled in business schools (Apling, 1993; Jung, 1980). Comparable statistics are difficult to determine, though estimates based on enrollment in accredited institutions suggest that the proportion is still approximately the same. Although enrollment in business fields has declined to approximately 20 percent for institutions accredited by the two main accreditors of the for-profit sector, the ACICS (Accrediting Council for Independent Colleges and Schools, 2004) and the ACCSCT (Accrediting Commission of Career Schools and Colleges of Technology, 2002), nearly every regionally accredited institution offers programs in business (Kinser, 2005d), accounting for nearly half of overall enrollment. It is reasonable to assume, then, that business continues to be among the more popular programs in the for-profit sector.

Other program categories continue to be present as well, though their proportions have shifted over the last decade or so. As in previous decades, cosmetology schools make up the largest proportion of institutions, though their numbers have declined and they enroll only about 10 percent of the students in the sector. Flight schools are less common now as well, likely because of tightening federal regulation of these institutions since the 1970s. Newspaper accounts suggest growing numbers of for-profit institutions moving into health fields and the expansion of their computer and technology programs (Floyd, 2005), and among regionally accredited for-profits, health and computer fields are the second and third most commonly offered programs (Kinser, 2005d). These areas are also at the top of the list of programs offered by institutions accredited by the Accrediting Council for Independent Colleges and Schools (2004) and the Accrediting Commission of Career Schools and Colleges of Technology (2002). A new category—education—is becoming more popular as for-profit institutions seek to tap into the demand for credentialed teachers and school administrators. The University of Phoenix, for example, reports 7 percent of its enrollment in education-related fields (Apollo Group, 2004). In addition to these disciplines, art remains popular, and a large proportion of institutions offers programs in paralegal studies, criminal justice, culinary arts, and tourism. Finally, at least two accredited for-profit law schools exist, and several institutions offer graduate degrees in psychology, most prominently Argosy University.

Degrees

For-profit degrees have been awarded since at least the 1950s (Miller and Hamilton, 1964; Petrello, 1987), though few details regarding the earliest degrees are known. The 1963 requirements of the Accrediting Commission for Business Schools, for example, limit the awarding of the baccalaureate degree to four years and 120 credit hours and associate degrees to two years and sixty credit hours (Miller and Hamilton, 1964). Several occupational degrees emerged in the late 1960s, including associate degrees in specialized technology, specialized business, and occupational studies, that required approximately eighteen hundred clock hours of instruction. At least nineteen for-profit schools had been certified to offer these awards in 1972 (Trivett, 1974). Department of Education data for that year (as analyzed by the author) identify thirty-six for-profit institutions with programs of two or more years in length, at least ten of which were degree-granting institutions (U.S. Department of Education, 1973). NCES began collecting data on "proprietary institutions of higher education" in 1976; the first count shows forty two-year and fifteen four-year for-profit schools (National Center for Education Statistics, 1991). The degree-granting status of these institutions is unclear, though it is likely that degree-granting for-profit institutions were underrepresented by the "institution of higher education" definition.[16] Still, they form a reasonable proxy of the number of collegiate-level for-profit institutions between 1976 and 1996, when NCES began reporting data for degree-granting institutions.

The proportion of collegiate institutions increased from under 3 percent to 7 percent of the total number of for-profit institutions by 1995, though much of the difference is the result of the steady decline in numbers of noncollegiate institutions beginning in the mid-1980s. Substantial growth in the number of degree-granting institutions occurred for the rest of the decade; in 2001, nearly one in five for-profit institutions had degree-granting authority. One should view these numbers with caution, however, when considering the general academic level of the education that occurs in the for-profit sector. Almost all for-profit institutions classified as "degree granting" also offer non-degree certificates, and some four-year institutions award more associate degrees than bachelor degrees (Bailey, Badway, and Gumport, 2003). To get a better sense of how the education being offered in the for-profit sector is changing, it is informative to look at degrees awarded (Table 3).

Table 3 shows the distribution of academic awards at Title IV for-profit institutions in 1996 and 2001. The total number of awards increased by 19 percent during this period, with the number of degrees more than

TABLE 3
Academic Awards at Title IV For-Profit Institutions in 1996 and 2001

	1996		2001		1996–2001
Nondegree	236,677	80.1%	232,028	66.0%	−2.0%
Associate	57,741	19.5%	77,743	22.1%	34.6%
Bachelor's	818	0.3%	26,398	7.5%	3,127.1%
Master's	224	0.1%	14,264	4.1%	6,267.9%
Doctorate	77	0.0%	656	0.2%	751.9%
Professional	62	0.0%	239	0.1%	285.5%
Total	295,599	100.0%	351,328	100.0%	18.9%

SOURCES: National Center for Education Statistics, 2000 (Table 173), and 2004b (Table 172).

doubling. The number of certificates actually declined by a modest 2 percent, but the proportion of certificates to degrees shifted dramatically from 80 percent of the awards in 1996 to 66 percent in 2001. The growth in the degree-granting function of for-profit higher education is stunning, though it is important to emphasize that the majority of awards in the sector are nondegree certificates and that the sector retains its overall vocational character.

Academic Models

It is not accurate to speak of a singular for-profit model any more than one can confidently assert the model employed by all not-for-profit private and public universities in the United States. Unlike traditional colleges and universities, however, very little is actually known about how for-profit institutions organize their curricular activities, design their courses, or determine when to add or subtract from the range of fields they teach. It was different in earlier eras. Along with information on the students, the owners, and the market in which for-profits operated, researchers often devoted substantial efforts to understanding the curriculum. Several dissertations on for-profit higher education dating back to 1939 address the academic organization of the for-profit business school (Miller and Hamilton, 1964). Most of the historical discussions of the sector include extensive descriptions of curriculum, including the structure and timing of the courses and programs offered (for example, Hayes and Jackson, 1935; Knepper, 1941; Reigner, 1959; Seybolt, 1971). Many of the major studies of for-profit education that were completed in the late 1960s and early 1970s likewise contain much information about the academic dimensions of the institutions they study. Belitsky (1969) outlines a range of admission standards, for example, and discusses how the for-profit schools in his study organize academic time. Hyde (1976) estimates profitability based on how the for-profit school delivers its curricular product. Wilms (1974) focuses substantial attention on an analysis of faculty workload.

A quarter century later, information such as these researchers provide is simply not available. In its place are found several studies that focus on the academic models at shareholder institutions and other degree-granting for-profit institutions. Even in an era where degree-granting institutions are becoming more important, it is embarrassing how little attention has been paid to the nondegree curricula that result in two-thirds of all academic credentials awarded in the sector. For example, nearly nine hundred cosmetology schools train more than 80,000 Title IV–eligible students in a highly regulated and competitive industry. Yet little effort has been made since Hyde's study (1976) in the early 1970s to understand how these institutions operate as centers of specialized knowledge. It is perhaps here where it is most clear how the limitations of the national datasets provided by the U.S. Department of Education have constrained the research agenda.

The academic policies and procedures of the degree-granting for-profit sector are slightly better known. Shareholder institutions such as the University of Phoenix and DeVry University have been most extensively studied (see Berg, 2005; Breneman, forthcoming; Kinser, 2005b; Kirp, 2003), and additional information is available from the reported practices of publicly traded corporations (Ruch, 2001, for example). The academic model that emerges from these analyses generally has five components:

Narrow mission—The focus of the curriculum is constrained both in terms of scope and purpose. For-profit schools prepare students for immediate employment in only a few fields and devote substantially all the curriculum to practical (rather than theoretical) instruction.

Limited faculty role—The faculty are not expected to conduct research or provide service to the institution. Nor do they participate in campus governance (though they may participate in curriculum development). They are hired to be teachers, whether in the classroom or online, and have few responsibilities beyond delivering the curriculum to students.

Centrally designed curriculum—Managers are responsible for deciding what is taught and how programs are to be organized, usually with external advisory boards and subject matter experts serving as consultants. Faculty make key decisions less often.

Standardization—Program variability is kept to a minimum. Students are given few choices regarding their program of study. The curriculum is mapped to specific outcomes, and grading is determined based on performance rubrics.

Economies of scale—Although substantial effort and financial resources are often required to design courses and programs, they are able to be replicated with limited additional expense. Successful curricula are rolled out as new products for other campuses in the corporate system.

Unfortunately, it is not known how widespread these components are outside the large shareholder universities. Some regionally accredited for-profit institutions, for example, have more traditional academic models, including broad faculty responsibility for the curriculum (Kinser, 2005d). The smaller institutions that remain outside large corporate ownership almost certainly would be less focused on economies of scale, and standardization likewise may be more commonly found in certain programs or institutions than in others. Even assumptions of a narrow mission do not hold for all institutions. At least two religious institutions, for example, converted to for-profit status while retaining their spiritual identity (Bartlett, 2005; Bollag, 2004), and accreditor-mandated general education requirements exist at most degree-granting institutions.

Admissions

The admission requirements at for-profit institutions have been a subject of regulatory interest, with particular concern directed toward the admission of students with limited ability to benefit from the instruction offered. The concern is that for-profit institutions will be reluctant to deny admission to students because they represent the revenue stream for the school. Ample historical evidence suggests that this concern is warranted (Fitzgerald and Harmon, 1988), and accusations of ongoing fraudulent admissions activities continue to dog the sector (Blumenstyk, 2004; Kroft, 2005; Phillips, 2004). One might thus assume that for-profit institutions have few admission requirements other than the ability to pay. The evidence suggests, however, that at least half the institutions in the sector have some standards for admission, including requiring applicants to provide some combination of test scores, previous academic records, demonstration of competency, or recommendations before being accepted into a program of study (National Center for Education Statistics, 2004b, Table 311). Admission requirements may be generally stricter in the for-profit sector than at community colleges because of the latter's widespread open-admission policies. For example, approximately 25 percent of the applicants at one for-profit campus are "out-placed" by entrance exams and other assessments that spot deficiencies below the academic minimum acceptable to the institution (Bailey, Badway, and Gumport, 2003, pp. 23–24).

One should be cautious in interpreting these findings too broadly. The comparison to community college admission standards sets the bar rather low. Four-year public and private not-for-profit institutions are less likely to be open-admission institutions and consequently would have substantially more extensive admission requirements than the for-profit sector. Moreover, the percentage of for-profit schools reporting admission requirements has declined—from 61 percent in 2000 to 51 percent in 2002—largely driven by the growing percentage of open-admission four-year for-profit institutions (National Center for Education Statistics, 2004b, Table 311). In addition, it is difficult to know the purpose of the admission requirements and the minimum qualifications expected from the applicant. It is possible that the requirements are quite modest and serve primarily to screen out plainly incapable applicants rather than as part of a selective admissions process. Finally, the existence of admission requirements does not eliminate the tension between the revenue-driven need to enroll students and the academic preparation needed to be successful in a technical program (Ruch, 2001, pp. 44–45). As student recruitment at the University of Phoenix was memorably described, getting "asses in classes" (Phillips, 2004) may still be a well-represented admissions policy in the for-profit sector.

Faculty

Teaching is central to the success of the for-profit sector. Unlike the curriculum, however, little attention historically has been paid to the instructors. In the earliest for-profit institutions, the owner was the sole faculty member, and instruction was based on self-produced textbooks. Later, additional instructors were hired from the ranks of recent graduates (Hayes and Jackson, 1935). Academic credentials did not become important until post–World War II accreditation agencies began to set standards. In 1939 only about 40 percent of the faculty held a bachelor's degree or higher; by 1963, 78 percent of the faculty in accredited business schools had earned an undergraduate degree, and nearly a quarter (23 percent) had completed an advanced degree (Miller and Hamilton, 1964). Estimates about the number of faculty can be found in data collected by the U.S. Office of Education until at least the 1940s (Bolino, 1973; U.S. Office of Education, 1942). The faculty ranks grew fairly steadily from a few hundred in 1870 to a prewar peak of six thousand in 1919, dropping to under four thousand on the eve of World War II. Women outnumbered men as instructors through much of this declining period, likely reflecting the changing curricular emphases that drew greater numbers of female students to the sector.

Belitsky's study (1969) contains the first empirical analysis of the instructional role of the for-profit faculty member. His account provides several items that continue to be relevant in considering faculty in the for-profit sector. The administrators of the for-profit school in the 1960s "are convinced that 'paper qualifications' are unimportant if an applicant for a teaching position knows his subject matter and can teach" (Belitsky, 1969, p. 81). Further, the supervision of instructors is fairly close and their curricular autonomy fairly low; student failure is equated with faculty failure. Tenure is not typically awarded, and although faculty members do little research, they do have substantial advising responsibilities.

Thirty-five years later, this description is still among the more complete ones of the for-profit faculty role. Whether it is still valid is less certain.

How Many?

With the growth in the number of degree-granting for-profit institutions, the number of faculty in the sector has increased substantially since the mid-1990s (Knapp and others, 2004; Roey, Skinner, Fernandez, and Barbett, 1999). In 2002 nearly 60,000 individuals served in a primarily instructional role, an increase of 63 percent since 1997. As Table 4 shows, the trend in the 1990s was away from full-time faculty in all sectors, though the for-profit sector overall relies substantially less on full-time faculty than do public and private not-for-profit institutions. Faculty model by level, however, differs greatly, with four out of five faculty at four-year institutions working part time, compared with an even split for two-year institutions and fewer than 40 percent for non-degree institutions. As Table 5 shows, community colleges actually employ a

TABLE 4
Percent of Full-Time Faculty, 1993–2002

Sector	1993	1997	2002
For-Profit	48.7	42.3	38.3
Public	58.8	57.0	53.0
Private, Not-for-Profit	61.3	62.1	55.6

SOURCES: Cahalan, Roey, Fernandez, and Barbett, 1996; Knapp and others, 2004; Roey, Skinner, Fernandez, and Barbett, 1999.

TABLE 5
Percent of Full-Time Faculty by Award Level, 2002

Award Level	For-Profit	Public	Private Not-for-Profit
Less Than Two Years	61.2	54.4	53.6
Two Years	50.3	32.6	50.8
Four Years	19.9	69.7	55.7

SOURCE: Knapp and others, 2004.

greater proportion of part-time faculty than do two-year for-profit institutions, and the proportion of full-time faculty at nondegree for-profit institutions is second only to that of public four-year colleges.

The common assertion, then, that for-profit institutions are dominated by part-time faculty seems to apply only to four-year for-profits rather than to the sector as a whole. And even this modest conclusion about faculty status is open to debate. Data available from shareholder owners suggest that the University of Phoenix faculty model skews the data. Table 6 shows faculty employed by selected publicly owned corporations. The Apollo Group, largely through the University of Phoenix, employs more than 17,000 part-time faculty, compared with just 362 full-time faculty. Among the owners listed, these numbers reduce the proportion of full-time faculty to 22.6 percent from 43.5 percent if Apollo faculty are not included. Because the University of Phoenix is counted as a four-year institution in NCES data, it could potentially account for half the total number of faculty and 70 percent of the part-time faculty at that level.[17] Without Phoenix, the proportion of full-time faculty for four-year institutions would be closer to 50 percent, similar to the ratio at for-profit two-year institutions and not dramatically different from the private, not-for-profit sector.

TABLE 6
Faculty Employed by Selected Publicly Owned Corporations

Owner	Full-Time Faculty	Part-Time Faculty	Percentage of Full-Time Faculty
Apollo	362	17,032	2.1
Career Education	2,091	3,009	41.0
Corinthian Colleges	1,476	1,663	47.0
DeVry	1,200	925	56.5
EDMC	1,654	2,391	40.9
ITT	893	948	48.5
Strayer	146	755	16.2
Total	7,822	2,6723	22.6
All but Apollo	7,460	9,691	43.5

SOURCE: SEC corporate filings.

TABLE 7
Student-Faculty Ratio by Award Level, 2002

Award Level	For-Profit	Public	Private Not-for-Profit
Less Than Two Years	13.6	4.6	5.6
Two Years	17.7	18.8	15.6
Four Years	13.0	15.7	10.3
All Levels	14.3	16.8	10.3

SOURCE: Knapp and others, 2004; National Center for Education Statistics, 2005.

Using faculty numbers for 2002 and the enrollment figures for the same year, it is possible to calculate the student-faculty ratio in the for-profit sector. Table 7 provides a comparison by level with public and private not-for-profit institutions. For-profit institutions in general have a student-faculty ratio of 14.3:1, compared with an overall ratio of 16.8:1 in the public sector and 10.3:1 in the private not-for-profit sector. Two- and four-year for-profit institutions have a lower student-faculty ratio than public institutions but a higher one than private not-for-profit colleges. Nondegree institutions, on the other hand, show a large disparity between the modest ratio in the for-profit sector and the rather low ratio in the public and private not-for-profit sectors. These data suggest that for-profit higher education provides adequate numbers of faculty to teach the students enrolled. Although this achievement may seem unremarkable at first glance, it is worth noting that the degree-granting for-profit sector has clearly been able to absorb a dramatic increase in enrollment over the last decade. Finding sufficient numbers of faculty has not, by this accounting, proved to be a barrier to growth.

What Is Their Role?

Comparisons of numbers of faculty and their employment status do little to indicate the differences between the job of a faculty member at a public or private not-for-profit institution and that of a for-profit faculty member. Descriptions of faculty life are limited in the recent literature, but almost all note that for-profit faculty devote nearly all their time to teaching, do not receive tenure, and have limited control over the curriculum (Breneman, forthcoming;

Kinser, 2005b; Kirp, 2003; Lechuga, 2004). In the for-profit sector, according to these accounts, the administration tells the faculty what they are to teach, and the faculty responsibility is to bring real-world experience into the classroom. Anecdotal evidence of administrative control suggests that it may be rather heavy-handed. Kirp (2003) tells how the faculty attempted to challenge a curricular decision made by DeVry managers. The result? "They lost," concludes Kirp succinctly and quotes the management philosophy: "The expectation is that [the faculty] will do it, like it or not" (2003, p. 248).

Most often, however, the faculty do like it and have little problem with the limited role they play (Breneman, forthcoming; Kelly, 2001; Kinser, 2005b; Lechuga, 2003). Three explanations for this apparent satisfaction are offered in the literature. First, the job is relatively easy. With syllabi provided and course outlines to guide the faculty member through each class, the effort required—intellectual or otherwise—is relatively modest (Breneman, forthcoming).[18] The second explanation is that the faculty enjoy teaching and are relieved of the additional responsibilities of research or governance that accompany a traditional faculty role (Kelly, 2001; Kinser, 2005b). The third reason for satisfaction in their job relates to a hiring process that brings in new faculty who fit the model. Doing so establishes a common faculty culture with few dissidents who might challenge the prevailing norms or be dissatisfied with the status quo (Kinser, 2005b; Lechuga, 2003).

The notion of for-profit faculty as part-time or "contingent" workers is another area of concern (Lechuga, 2004). The lack of job protection through tenure, uncertain institutional commitment to academic freedom, and limited participation in institutional governance may create an academic workforce that is segregated from traditional higher education norms and values. But the connection from contingency to segregation is not as straightforward as it may seem. Whereas contingent faculty in public and private not-for-profit higher education are often considered second-class citizens, in the for-profit sector, they are central to the success of the institutions where they work. The part-time faculty at the University of Phoenix, for example, are not considered adjuncts as they would be at a traditional institution. Rather they are the real faculty and function with pride as the instructional core of the University (Breneman, forthcoming). Thus, it may be difficult to evaluate the for-profit faculty member against a standard established in the public and private not-for-profit sectors. The relatively low proportion of full-time to part-time faculty, for example, almost certainly does not have the same meaning in a community college as it does in a four-year for-profit college. At the same time, some aspects of the for-profit faculty role—specifically the focus on teaching—may provide an important lens through which to view the multiple and often conflicting faculty roles at the traditional college or university (Breneman, 2005; Kinser, 2005b).

The modern descriptions of for-profit faculty life are remarkably similar to those described in the 1960s (Belitsky, 1969), even as the sector has changed dramatically in the intervening years. This fact may suggest that the basic economics of for-profit higher education constrain the faculty role irrespective of institutional size, curriculum, delivery methods, or degree level. The current accounts are limited, however, making such a conclusion questionable. Most are primarily based on case study analyses of the University of Phoenix (Breneman, forthcoming; Kinser, 2005b) and DeVry University (Kirp, 2003), and these models are likely atypical. Moreover, although it is clear that for-profit faculty, in general, have instruction as their primary focus, it is too simplistic to contrast that with the trinity of teaching, research, and service presumably performed by faculty in traditional colleges and universities. National and international surveys of traditional faculty show much variation in what faculty actually do, with a sizable proportion reporting teaching as the primary—and preferred—occupation (Forest, 2002). Without research of comparable detail on faculty in the for-profit sector, it is possible to make only limited observations from the available data.

Do Students Learn?

One of the claims proponents of for-profit higher education frequently make is that the academic models employed by these institution are directed toward the ways adults learn (see Ruch, 2001; Sperling and Tucker, 1997). Small classes, self-directed and active learning, practical application of knowledge, and discussion-based instruction are considered the hallmarks of the for-profit sector and are regularly cited as principles of good practice in adult learning. Given this situation, for-profit institutions ought to be—in theory at least—places where quality learning takes place. The evidence that it does, however, is sparse. Little is known about the learning outcomes of for-profit higher education or the effectiveness of nontraditional teaching models employed by some of the larger for-profit institutions.[19] Assessments of students' intellectual development in the for-profit sector are nonexistent. And almost nothing is known about what actually happens in the for-profit classroom as opposed to what faculty training manuals and campus administrators claim is occurring.

That reality might fall short of the rhetoric is certainly the impression left by Kirp's account (2003, pp. 243–245) of DeVry University classrooms. In a general education class, the students have not read the assignment, and despite the instructor's valiant efforts to engage them, they remain uninterested in the material. In a technical class, however, the students are prepared, taking notes and working the problems assigned by the instructor. The difference is not in the academic model or the quality of the teaching, asserts Kirp, but rather that the technical class provides information students need to get a job. At DeVry, as elsewhere, it can be a challenge to get students to see general education classes as worthwhile, and little in the literature suggests that the for-profit institution is any more successful in its efforts than the public college down the road. But are they less successful? Some would say "yes." As was mentioned in the chapter on students, the for-profit sector does not do a particularly good job of facilitating transfer to higher degrees, and, even in four-year institutions, a relatively small proportion actually earn bachelor degrees or higher. Other research shows that the social benefits of postsecondary education may elude students in the for-profit sector (Persell and Wenglinsky, 2004). Because these institutions are so focused on providing job-related skills, the higher purpose of education may be given short shrift. The not-so-subtle message to students such as those Kirp (2003) observed is that general education does not, in fact, matter much at all.

This latter point has caused some to suggest that most institutions in the sector should not be considered "higher education" at all. Making a broader point about institutions with narrow curricula and a training focus, Altbach (2001) labels them "pseudo-universities" and argues that classifying them with traditional colleges cheapens the broad liberal education that should characterize true higher education. The for-profit sector often faces questions of legitimacy (Kinser, 2004a), and many are uncomfortable putting a for-profit school on a par with a major research university. To question the extent of higher learning (as opposed to "lower" learning or mere training) in the for-profit sector, however, requires empirical evidence that is thus far lacking. Rather than further rhetorical arguments, the paucity of data on student learning should inspire researchers to address this gap in the literature.

External Approval: Accrediting the For-Profit Sector

R ELATED TO THE CHANGING ACADEMIC MISSION of for-profit institutions is the development of an accreditation system for the external approval and validation of the sector. Accreditation has not been a significant issue in the for-profit sector during most of its history. Owners of institutions that trained students for career-specific occupations traditionally believed that an employed graduate was the only stamp of approval they needed. That situation started to change in the federal student aid era after World War II, when accreditation became a precondition for eligibility for aid. In the 1970s and 1980s, accreditation became much more common as the scope of the federal student aid programs expanded, and by the beginning of the Wall Street era, accreditation was a key indicator of a legitimate postsecondary institution, particularly of the growing number of degree-granting institutions. Today, almost all degree-granting for-profit institutions, and close to half of all nondegree for-profits, are accredited by an agency recognized by the U.S. Department of Education (Kinser, 2005a).

Because of their relatively late arrival to accredited status and their numeric minority in the degree-granting postsecondary universe, for-profit institutions have faced discrimination in accreditation agencies dominated by the nonprofit sectors. Regional accreditors, in particular, have resisted including for-profit institutions as members, and some specialized accreditors have taken steps to discourage for-profit institutions from submitting their programs for review. As voluntary membership organizations, accreditation agencies have the right to restrict membership as long as they follow their own procedures and do not violate federal antitrust provisions

(Kaplan and Lee, 1995). As gatekeepers to the financial aid system in the United States, however, they are under pressure to base their membership decisions on educational criteria rather than ownership status. These once categorical prohibitions against for-profit higher education have slowly crumbled, and accreditors of all stripes have accepted for-profit institutions and programs in their ranks, albeit reluctantly. The transformations discussed in this chapter, then, are not only about the for-profit sector. The accreditors have changed as well to accommodate the development and expansion of profit-making institutions.

Background on Accreditation

Accreditation in the United States is distinctive and somewhat confusing. Rather than having a centralized government ministry as is the case in many other countries, private nongovernmental accreditation organizations have assumed much responsibility for the postsecondary system. Two distinct types of accreditation exist: (1) specialized accreditation is designed to evaluate particular programs based on standards established by academics and professionals in that field; and (2) institutional accreditation evaluates the operation of an entire institution, generally assessing whether the college or school as a whole meets standards agreed upon by the member institutions.

Specialized accreditation applies to for-profit and not-for-profit private and public institutions similarly. In fact, because many "specializations" are directly connected to credentialing necessary to be eligible for employment, the for-profit sector has been an active participant in specialized accreditation, though it is unclear whether discrimination toward the sector from the nonprofit educational community has been lessened as a result.

Institutional accreditation, on the other hand, exhibits a bifurcation between for-profit institutions, which are generally accredited by national agencies, and nonprofit institutions, which are generally accredited by regional associations. Most of the more than fifty national accrediting associations focus on a specific type of school (such as business, art, law, or distance education) and accredit both degree- and non-degree-granting institutions. Memberships of some national accreditors are dominated by institutions from the for-profit sector—the National Accrediting Commission of Cosmetology Arts and Sciences, for example—while about one-third of them, such as the American Academy for Liberal Education, do not accredit any for-profit institutions at all. The system of regional accreditation divides the United States into six geographic regions based on state borders. Each regional association is responsible for accrediting all eligible degree-granting institutions within its region and non-U.S. institutions that request U.S. accreditation. The regions are different sizes—from the North Central region, which covers nineteen states in the Midwest and southwest, to the Western region, which has authority over just two states, California and Hawaii. Not-for-profit private and public institutions make up the vast majority of regionally accredited institutions, with less than 5 percent of their membership coming from the for-profit sector (Kinser, 2005d). A few for-profit institutions hold both regional and national accreditation. In most of those cases, the institution is transitioning from national to regional accreditation, or the national agency also serves as a specialized accreditor (for example, the Accrediting Bureau of Health Education Schools also accredits allied health programs).

Institutional accreditation—regional or national—is one of the pillars of eligibility for federal financial aid. Accreditation agencies must be recognized by the U.S. Department of Education for their members to participate in federal aid programs. From the perspective of public policy, then, it makes no difference whether an institution is accredited by a national or regional association. From a practical perspective, however, nationally accredited institutions are often viewed as second-class citizens of the higher education community, while regional accreditation has been traditionally perceived as an indicator of quality and status (Kinser, 2004a). Regionally accredited institutions often look askance on the transfer of credits from nationally accredited institutions, for example, and no nationally accredited institution is a member of the prestigious Association of American Universities or ranked in the high-profile *U.S. News & World Report* annual college guide. The historical and cultural basis of this prejudice awaits future scholarship, though it is clear that the for-profit sector, as the main participant in national accreditation, has a particular interest in challenging this reality (Kinser, 2004a).

History

For-profit institutions have been accredited almost as long as their cousins in the public and private not-for-profit sectors. Following a broad educational trend toward self-regulation, regional accreditation agencies were established for nonprofit colleges and universities by the early 1900s (Alstete, 2004), and the New York State Board of Regents had established accreditation procedures for several for-profit colleges around the same time (Herrick, 1904). Accreditation agencies for the for-profit sector emerged in the 1910s and 1920s. Business schools established the National Association of Accredited Commercial Schools in 1912 (Petrello, 1987), an association for barber and beauty schools was organized in 1924 (American Association of Cosmetology Schools, 2005), and the National Home Study Council was created to serve correspondence schools in 1926 (Bolino, 1973). These organizations were concerned with maintaining quality in the for-profit sector and established standards that member institutions were required to meet. They operated side by side with the more prominent regional associations before World War II, apparently even accrediting some of the same institutions (Petrello, 1987).[20] This common agenda faded, however, and by midcentury, all regional associations categorically denied recognition to for-profit degree-granting institutions.

After World War II, the GI bill supported the educational pursuits of returning veterans. The original strategy for identifying eligible institutions—authorization by the states—proved inadequate to the task of preventing students from wasting their money on fraudulent schools. The U.S. Office of Education began recognizing accreditation agencies for the purpose of determining eligibility to participate in GI bill programs in 1952. Because they were essentially prevented from gaining regional accreditation, for-profit business and correspondence schools adapted their existing accreditation bodies to meet the new federal requirements. The Accrediting Commission for Business Schools was recognized in 1956, and the National Home Study Council was recognized in 1959 (U.S. Department of Education, 2004). Still, most for-profit institutions remained outside the accreditation process, and external oversight of the sector was minimal (Hamilton, 1958).

The passage of the Higher Education Act in 1965 made available more federal money for student aid, and accreditation was once again placed in the role of gatekeeper. Barber and beauty schools, trade and technical schools, and schools of allied health each modified existing professional associations to comply with the federal guidelines for new recognition as approved accreditation agencies. With the recognition in 1978 of the Accrediting Council for Continuing Education and Training, all of today's major national accrediting associations for for-profit higher education (see Table 8) were in operation. Unaccredited for-profit institutions of higher education became less common, particularly for the growing number of degree-granting institutions. The explicit linking of federal financial aid to institutional accreditation encouraged the notoriously independent proprietary school operator to acquiesce to external review of his or her school. Reputable owners finally claimed success in their longstanding call for

TABLE 8
Number of For-Profit Institutions Accredited by Major National Accrediting Associations

| Accrediting Agency | Number at Award Level | | | Percentage of For-Profit Institutions |
	Four	Two	Less Than Two	
National Accrediting Commission of Cosmetology Arts and Sciences	0	177	689	84.5
Accrediting Commission of Career Schools and Colleges of Technology	53	223	334	79.0
Accrediting Council for Independent Colleges and Schools	131	244	107	78.6
Council on Occupational Education	2	37	115	32.1
Accrediting Council for Continuing Education and Training	0	15	78	86.9
Accrediting Bureau of Health Education Schools	5	58	78	62.9

SOURCE: Kinser, 2005a.

accreditation as a means of weeding out the fraudulent institutions that have historically been the bane of the for-profit sector (Hamilton, 1958; Jones, 1973; Miller and Hamilton, 1964; Petrello, 1987). Their claims were rather premature, as the scandals described elsewhere in this volume attest. Nevertheless, since the 1970s accreditation has become widely accepted in the for-profit sector. Shortly after passage of the 1972 reauthorization of the Higher Education Act, it was estimated that only 10 to 15 percent of for-profit institutions were accredited (Jones, 1973).[21] Now, nearly all degree-granting and around half of the nondegree for-profit institutions are accredited by an agency recognized by the U.S Department of Education (Kinser, 2005a).

Regional Accreditation

Even with the opportunities provided by national accreditors that allowed for-profit institutions to access federal aid, the sector remained closed off from the regional associations until the 1970s. Postwar regional accreditation was overtly hostile to for-profit higher education. More precisely, the profit motive in general was seen as an unseemly intrusion into the eleemosynary traditions of higher education, not to be tolerated. The 1967 case of Parsons College (Koerner, 1970b) is a good example of how a regional accreditor reacted to the rejection of the nonprofit ethos of its membership. The North Central Association closely scrutinized and ultimately disaccredited the private not-for-profit college in Iowa for (among other things) operating with the aim of maximizing revenue, even as it acknowledged that it had quality faculty and that its teaching model and student counseling were praiseworthy. A particular bone of contention was the college president's insistence on using the word "profit" to describe his financial model for the institution (Koerner, 1970b). Parsons College sued the North Central Association in federal court. The judge in the case ruled in favor of the accreditor, stating that "rudimentary due process" was provided and declining to consider or evaluate the merit of the association's accreditation standards (Kaplan and Lee, 1995).

The first case involving the regional accreditation of a for-profit institution followed on the heels of the Parsons College case (Kaplan, 1971; Koerner, 1970a). In 1966 Marjorie Webster Junior College, a for-profit women's college in Washington, D.C., applied for accreditation from the Middle States Association. The school's application was rejected without evaluation or consideration because, as a for-profit institution, it did not meet Middle States eligibility requirements. Marjorie Webster sued, and in a sweeping decision the District Court ruled in favor of the proprietary school. The court stated that denying accreditation solely on the basis of the profit-making status of the institutions was an unreasonable restraint of trade. The monopoly status of Middle States in its region and the "quasi-governmental" nature of regional accreditation created an opening for the court to intervene in a private organization's membership decisions. The victory was short-lived, however, as the court of appeals overturned the lower court's decision less than a year later. Significantly, however, the appeals court did not reject the lower court's legal conclusion that it could intervene in the decisions of an accrediting body, only that in the circumstances of this case, the Middle States decision should be accorded deference (Kaplan, 1971).

It was a Pyrrhic victory for regional accreditation. Even the language of the appeals court suggested that the days of judicial deference were quickly coming to a close. As Kaplan (1971) states in his contemporaneous review of the case, the monopolistic nature of accreditation agencies became part of the legal debate, and the concept of accreditation as a quasi-governmental activity means that constitutional requirements of due process apply. Some regional accreditors saw the writing on the wall and began to make changes. In 1971, the Southern Association of Schools and Colleges established a separate accreditation commission for nondegree occupational schools, some of which were for-profit trade schools (Council on Occupational Education, 2004). Other regional associations moved to admit for-profit institutions as regular members, including Middle States (Van Dyne, 1974). Unfortunately for Marjorie Webster, however, these decisions came too late. The owners sold the school shortly after they lost on appeal, and it closed a few years later (Van Dyne, 1974).

The first for-profit institutions to go through regional accreditation certainly had to face skeptical evaluators to gain admission as full members. It is not clear, however, the extent to which the institutions' profit-making status was always the primary issue. The story of the University of Phoenix's encounter with the regional Western association, for example, has been colorfully told by the university's founder, John Sperling (2000). Sperling's account describes a vindictive accrediting staff attempting to sabotage his fledgling for-profit venture. The University of Phoenix was therefore established in Arizona rather than in California, where it would be evaluated by the North Central Association, a more amenable regional accreditor that resisted the pressure to deny accreditation from the other five associations. This story should be viewed with a healthy grain of salt. Despite Sperling's claim to be the first regionally accredited for-profit institution, at least eight other for-profit institutions had been accredited by three other regional associations before Phoenix's 1978 reward (Kinser, 2005d). In fact, the Western Association, the object of Sperling's published attack, had accredited two for-profit institutions and was in the process of evaluating a third when Phoenix applied to North Central. North Central, on the other hand, had not accredited any for-profit institutions at the time (Kinser, 2005d), and its actions during the Parsons College case a decade earlier could hardly have suggested that it would be a more accommodating region. Sperling's engaging history (2000) notwithstanding, it seems reasonable to suspect that it was the nontraditional structure and unique academic model of the University of Phoenix rather than its profit-making status that caused such a ruckus.

After the regional associations digested the *Marjorie Webster* case, few instances occurred of apparent resistance to for-profit membership. The Southern Association provides a partial exception in its accreditation battle with Sullivan Junior College (Friedlander, 1980). Having established an openness to accrediting nondegree for-profit institutions through its commission on occupational education, it drew the line in 1978 on accrediting the degree-granting Sullivan. Only after the school threatened to sue did the association relent and decide to accredit the Kentucky institution as well as a for-profit art school in Florida. No court cases have tested the *Marjorie Webster* decision with respect to the regional accreditors, though from the reaction of the Southern Association in the Sullivan case, it seems that the regional accreditors were reluctant to press their luck.

The regional associations may have been reluctant for another reason. As early as 1972, the U.S. Office of Education began questioning the basis for prohibiting for-profit institutional accreditation (Coughlin, 1977). Regardless of whether the accreditors had legal justification for restricting their membership, the government hinted strongly that continued recognition as an approved accreditor would require an openness to for-profit institutional membership. Accreditation agencies relied on federal recognition to provide their membership with access to financial aid. If that recognition were withdrawn, then a prime benefit would be lost—which may have been an empty threat. The regional accreditors had a long history and a strong institutional base that arguably would have been able to thwart such a move by the federal government, particularly when the for-profit sector at the time (mid-1970s) still largely consisted of rather marginal educational institutions. The accrediting council of the American Bar Association actually faced down that threat in the late 1970s (Coughlin, 1977) and, after a brief study period, maintained its ban on accrediting for-profit law schools. Still, with the skepticism of the judicial branch weighing on their minds, the regional associations may have wanted to avoid scrutiny by the executive branch as well.

Debates about regional accreditation of for-profit higher education continued through the 1980s without much widespread agreement (Kerins, 1989; Thompson, 1989). In the 1990s, the broader question of whether an accrediting body could refuse to accredit a for-profit institution was addressed in an antitrust lawsuit filed by the U.S. Department of Justice against the American Bar Association (ABA) (U.S. Department of Justice, 1995). Although the suit was primarily about how the accrediting process was used to prop up faculty salaries and benefits, the agreement that settled the case specifically prohibited the ABA's accreditation committee from denying recognition to a school simply because it operated for profit. The case resonated within the accreditation community (Leatherman, 1995) and perhaps spurred more for-profit institutions to seek regional accreditation. But even as more for-profit institutions sought and gained membership, regional accreditors remained aloof to the idea of accrediting for-profit institutions. As late as 2001, the president of the Council for Higher Education Accreditation noted that regional accreditors had yet to tackle the issues surrounding the accreditation of for-profit higher education (Eaton, 2001). Unlike the rise of distance education, the growth of the for-profit sector has caused little reflection among the regional accreditors (Alstete, 2004). It is clear that regional accreditors can no longer exclude for-profit higher education from their associations, and a real expansion of regionally accredited for-profit higher education is occurring (Kinser, 2005d). The impact of this new reality on regional accreditation, however, is not yet so clear.

For-Profit Accrediting Agencies

Thirty national and seven regional agencies accredit for-profit institutions of higher education (Kinser, 2004b, 2005a, 2005d). The seven regional agencies together accredit about seventy separate institutions, or about 2 percent of their membership. Primarily because several of the accredited for-profit schools are rather large with multiple campuses, regional accreditation is actually quite widespread in the for-profit sector. In 2004, 428 locations in forty-two states, Puerto Rico, and the District of Columbia had regional accreditation, enrolling nearly half of all students in for-profit degree-granting institutions. National agencies, on the other hand, are responsible for roughly twice as many degree-granting campuses and all the non-degree-granting institutions. As Table 8 shows, most for-profit institutions are accredited by just six national agencies, and only five have a majority of their total membership from the for-profit sector.

The difference between regional and national accreditation causes problems for students who wish to transfer credits between a nationally accredited and a regionally accredited institution. It has become an issue for the for-profit sector and has motivated some for-profit campuses to seek regional accreditation (Kinser, 2005d). Regional accreditors, however, do not prohibit credit transfer from national accreditors; policies are set by individual institutions. Even so, in a system of higher education marked by high student mobility, accreditation status plays an important role in determining the future academic opportunities of for-profit students. Particularly considering that most for-profits award two-year degrees, the ability to transfer to other institutions may be an important factor in student recruitment. The inability to transfer, on the other hand, could help explain the low rate of attaining a bachelor's degree by graduates of two-year for-profit schools.

Some for-profit institutions are accredited by more than one accrediting agency, but it is unusual for a school to hold accreditation by more than one of the six main institutional accreditors or from a regional accreditor and one of the main national accreditors. This practice was apparently more common when for-profit institutions first started seeking accreditation, but it attracted some criticism from those who suggested that dual accreditation was illegitimately being used to mask institutional problems (Young, 1987). Problems that attracted the attention of one accrediting agency could be hidden from a second agency, thus maintaining institutional eligibility while the issue was being resolved. All accreditors now require institutions to disclose any changes of accreditation status,[22] and the federal government requires that accreditors immediately review the accreditation status of any member that has a change in status (U.S. Department of Education, 1999). Perhaps because of these changes, dual accreditation no longer seems to be an issue in the for-profit sector.

All accrediting agencies that accredit for-profit institutions also accredit non-profit institutions. For most agencies, in fact, not-for-profit private and public institutions make up the majority of their membership. Whether this status affects the standards employed by the agencies or their interpretation of them with respect to their minority for-profit membership is not known. The only sub-stantial investigation focused on regional accreditors. The Education Commission of the States (ECS) (2000) found that although regional associations have few standards specifically directed toward for-profit institutions, they typically apply their rules differently in evaluating the for-profit sector. The accreditors reported paying closer attention to governance and financial arrangements in the for-profit sector. Because the ECS did not link the accreditation practices to the specific policies of the regional association, it is not clear the extent to which this additional focus represents actual differences in application or interpretation as opposed to heightened awareness of potential problems based on experience. At any rate, no regional accreditor specifically states that it will apply its rules differently depending on the profit-making status of the institutions, and some specifically preclude this option. The Southern Association of Schools and Colleges, for example, says, "The Commission on Colleges applies the requirements of its *Principles* to all applicant, candidate, and member institutions, regardless of the type of institution; private for-profit, private not-for-profit, or public"

(Commission on Colleges, 2001, p. 7). Unfortunately, no investigation—even one as limited as the ECS study (2000)—has been completed of accrediting standards for the national accrediting agencies.[23]

Regional Accreditation of National Institutions

National institutions have campuses in multiple states or are virtual universities. Although a few private not-for-profit institutions have a national presence, for-profit higher education has a long history of growth through multiple branch campuses and other expansion efforts. The intersection of this organizational growth strategy and the concept of accreditation based on geographic regions pose some difficulties. Two main problems are readily apparent. The first is how to account for an institution that is accredited under the standards of one region yet is operating in another region. A simple solution to this issue would be the standardization of accreditation policies to eliminate regional variation. Some steps along these lines were taken with the accreditation bid of the not-for-profit Western Governors University and the subsequent creation of the Council of Regional Accrediting Commissions (Kinser, 2002b). As a result, specific policies regarding the accreditation of cross-regional institutions have been adopted in each region. These policies generally place the responsibility for accreditation on the home region while preserving the right of the host region to be notified of and participate in the accreditation process. Although no formal process exists for resolving a dispute between the home and host regions about a particular institution, the policies seem to anticipate a collegial response to any concerns raised.

The resolution to the first problem recognizes that regional variability in standards may be a concern. The response, however, is directed primarily toward the accreditation community rather than the institution at the heart of the matter. The second problem, then, is how to prevent such a cross-regional institution from "shopping" for the most accommodating region from which to seek accreditation. And some evidence exists that such shopping occurs. John Sperling's account (2000) of his battles with the Western Association suggest his motive for moving the University of Phoenix to Arizona was to avoid further confrontations with the California accreditor. Walden University notes in its history that the for-profit distance learning institution moved to Minnesota in 1982 because it felt its chances of receiving regional accreditation were better in that state (Walden University, 2003). More recently, another for-profit online institution, the American Public University System, moved its headquarters to West Virginia in 2002 after being turned down in a bid for recognition from the Southern Association in Virginia (Barker, 2004). The differences in regional standards leaves the system vulnerable to some enterprising owners who may look for an edge to gain the mark of distinction regional accreditation implies. As yet no real solution to this problem exists.

The issue of accreditation shopping deserves further attention, however, as every instance cited above represents an institution choosing to move to the North Central Association's region to gain regional accreditation. It leads one to wonder whether the North Central region is the place to go for the accreditation of multistate or virtual for-profit institutions of higher education. Quite unlike the other regional accreditors, the North Central Association has become a "national regional" accrediting body for for-profit higher education (Kinser, 2004b). More than half of the for-profit campuses accredited by the agency are actually located outside the region. In fact, North Central accredits more for-profit institutions in the Northwest and Western regions than do the commissions in those regions. Much of the out-of-region presence of the North Central Association is the responsibility of the huge University of Phoenix system—Phoenix has more campuses outside the North Central region than it has inside the region—but almost all the out-of-region campuses of other for-profit institutions also have North Central accreditation. All regionally accredited virtual universities and half the major distance education providers also hold accreditation from the North Central Association (Kinser, 2005d). As a consequence, the region has become a significant net exporter of for-profit higher education to other parts of the country.

A well-circulated witticism attributed to Mary Burgan, executive director of the American Association of University Professors, suggests that the North Central Association would accredit a ham sandwich; with cheese it could grant a master's degree. A less provocative commentator might suggest that North Central's standards are insufficient to ensure quality higher education. A more neutral observation, however, is perhaps warranted. As indicated earlier, no complete analyses have been done of the accrediting standards of the various regions, but the observed outcome suggests that North Central is, in fact, doing something different. Kinser's analysis (2004b) of institutional eligibility requirements related to this question shows that North Central has the fewest number of requirements and that they are briefer and stated in more general terms than are the requirements of other regional associations. Although eligibility applies to all institutions, for-profit and non-profit alike, the impression is that a wider variety of institutions are considered eligible for accreditation under North Central's guidelines. Several nontraditional for-profit institutions seem to have—quite appropriately—taken advantage of that openness and flexibility to gain regional accreditation. Whether this tactic represents the nationalization of regional accreditation remains to be seen.

Creating the Playing Field: State and Federal Regulation

A LONG WITH THE WIDESPREAD ACCREDITATION of for-profit institutions, state and federal regulations create the playing field on which profit-making institutions compete with other institutions of higher education. One marker of the current regulatory environment is the growing integration of the for-profit sector into the same regulatory framework that applies to traditional not-for-profit private and public higher education. The expansion of the for-profit sector, the development of degree-granting for-profit universities, and the creation of the large publicly traded institutions of the Wall Street era have occurred in this increasingly integrated environment.

All of which does not mean, however, that the regulatory playing field is level. Substantial differences remain within a common framework. Regulation of for-profit higher education is primarily a state function, with a significant role for the federal government and nongovernmental accrediting bodies—essentially the same triad that oversees the private not-for-profit and public postsecondary sectors. In practice, however, the for-profit sector often faces different regulatory pressures. As discussed in the previous chapter, for-profit institutions rely primarily on national accrediting bodies, as opposed to the regional accreditors most common in the public and private not-for-profit realms. At the state level, for-profit institutions still may be considered a special case of postsecondary education and regulated separately from more traditional institutions. At the federal level, for-profit higher education is singled out in the Higher Education Act and must meet distinct requirements that do not apply to other institutions. Moreover, regulation of the sector also occurs through bodies not typically associated with higher education, namely the

Federal Trade Commission (FTC) and the SEC. Finally, some institutions in the for-profit sector exist outside the regulatory structure that governs most legitimate postsecondary institutions. Many of these institutions are fraudulent diploma mills, in which case consumer protection regulations apply as they would for any business enterprise. Much like the accreditation of the for-profit sector, a full analysis of the regulatory environment for for-profit higher education has not been completed.

State Oversight

To the extent that the for-profit sector historically was regulated, it came at the state level. Little direct federal involvement occurred until the 1970s, and independent accrediting bodies did not emerge until the 1950s. Even among the states, regulation was rather limited through the middle of the twentieth century. Before that time, the literature contains few examples of state involvement in the for-profit sector other than recognizing their existence as business enterprises.[24] Massachusetts in 1888 was the first state to propose licensing all for-profit institutions, but the proposal never became law (Fulton, 1969). A little more than a decade later, New York State began exercising control over some aspects of the sector, primarily through inspections and examinations by the state Board of Regents (James, 1900). A noted example of the power uniquely assumed by New York was the issuance of a restraining order preventing a for-profit school from using the word "university" in its name (Herrick, 1904). Other states followed New York's lead and explicitly acknowledged the rights of proprietors to establish educational institutions as business enterprises. Some states chose only to license schools—in other words, they gave a permit to an owner to operate the school with few substantive requirements—while others adopted a certification model that implies greater scrutiny of curriculum, faculty, finances, and academic policies (Fulton, 1969).

For the first half of the twentieth century, however, most states sat on the sidelines, adopting a laissez-faire attitude toward the for-profit sector. In the 1950s, just seventeen states had any provision for the licensing, approval, or registration of these institutions (Hamilton, 1958). The lack of effective oversight at the state level caused substantial difficulties after World War II with the influx of federal money from GI bill students. The National Education Association (NEA) attempted to draft sample legislation for state adoption that would establish and standardize licensure rules for the for-profit sector, but no consensus could be reached (Hamilton, 1958). State oversight continued to be problematic through the 1960s, even as more states passed laws concerning for-profit institutions. The majority of state policies of the 1960s and early 1970s, however, were grounded in consumer protection concerns rather than the maintenance of educational quality (Trivett, 1974). Advertising, for example, was often more stringently regulated in the for-profit sector than among not-for-profit private and public institutions, while suitable levels of academic work and instructional time were only minimally addressed. By 1972, the majority of the states had laws on the books regulating for-profit institutions (Trivett, 1974) but often under business codes rather than as part of the educational system.

The federal reauthorization of the Higher Education Act in 1972 forced the states to take the for-profit schools seriously as educational institutions. The legislation required new state commissions that specifically included representatives from the for-profit sector. Regulatory issues were pressing, and the ECS in 1973 took on the task of drafting model legislation that the NEA had abandoned in the 1950s. Minimum standards were suggested in application information, catalog content, admission policies, instructional materials, record keeping, advertising and sales, placement rates, tuition refunds, facilities, faculty, support staff, and financial viability. The states were much more receptive this time, and the ECS model became a key resource for revising or establishing new laws (Chaloux, 1985; Schenet, 1990). The focus, however, continued to be on policing behavior and preventing fraud. State laws generally covered only minimal standards for educational quality while maintaining strict rules over ethics, fiscal responsibility, and advertising.

Several conferences and meetings were held in the 1970s and early 1980s to address concerns about state regulatory efforts, but other than the ECS contribution of model legislation, little progress was made toward further reform (Chaloux, 1985). The for-profit sector was generally excluded from state postsecondary planning and was regulated by a diverse set of state agencies. Non-degree-granting for-profit institutions in particular existed in a separate regulatory environment from not-for-profit private and public institutions. Although forty-three states and the District of Columbia had some sort of licensure or authorization procedure in the mid-1980s, perhaps only thirty-eight had actual oversight responsibilities that go beyond simple registration or accreditation requirements (Chaloux, 1985).[25] The states were, however, beginning to recognize a distinctive degree-granting for-profit sector and started to use criteria oriented toward educational validity of the activity for these institutions as compared with nondegree institutions (Chaloux, 1985).

The explosive growth of degree-granting for-profit higher education a decade later led the ECS to once again delve into the issue of state regulation (Brimah, 2000). Looking at a sample of eleven states, the ECS determined that degree-granting for-profit institutions participate in essentially the same state regulatory structure as more traditional colleges and universities. In six of the states, all private higher education—for-profit and not-for-profit—was considered similarly by a single agency, while in four states, public sector institutions were also included under the agency's regulatory authority. Only one state considered for-profit institutions a separate agency. Following the pattern established in the 1980s, educational issues account for a substantial component of the regulatory attention for degree-granting institutions. Maintaining educational coherence, the faculty's academic qualifications, and adequate library facilities—in addition to the more prosaic concern with licensing applications and financial stature—were common requirements across the states. Few differences were apparent in the procedures applied to for-profit institutions, and most states in the study did not even identify the profit-making status of the institutions they reviewed (Brimah, 2000).

The ECS analysis, while the most recent available, is nonetheless limited. Only states with large for-profit sectors were selected to participate; states known for historically lax regulation of the for-profit sector (such as Hawaii, Mississippi, and Wyoming) were not assessed. In addition, by reviewing only rules pertaining to degree-granting institutions, the significant population of nondegree for-profit institutions is neglected. Its broad conclusions regarding the lack of bias against for-profit institutions in state regulations should therefore be viewed with caution.

The differences in state regulations between the 1980s and 1990s, however, do show that the degree-granting for-profit sector is becoming better integrated into the broader higher education regulatory structures in the states. A state-by-state comparison of the licensure and approval agencies compiled in an ECS database (2005) of postsecondary governance structures with the state oversight bodies listed (Chaloux, 1985) suggests that the trend may be extending to non-degree-granting institutions as well. Of the fifty states and the District of Columbia, twenty-two have adopted new regulatory structures that place for-profit institutions under oversight with their not-for-profit peers, while six have changed policies to segregate them from other institutions. It is still quite common, however, to differentiate institutions by their degree status. Because more for-profit nondegree institutions exist, de facto segregation may continue, with the majority of the for-profit presence in the state being regulated by a separate agency rather than the one that regulates most public and private not-for-profit institutions. Nevertheless, a trend toward inclusion seems evident, and the majority of states no longer place different sectors under separate regulatory agencies. Outright prohibition is even more rare, with only one state—Rhode Island—excluding degree-granting for-profit higher education from operating within its borders (Education Commission of the States, 2005; Rhode Island Board of Governors for Higher Education, 2004).

That said, some states may continue to treat for-profit institutions differently, even when the regulatory structures are the same. As the ECS (2000) noted in its analysis of regional accreditation of the for-profit sector, placing all postsecondary institutions under a common framework may still result in a different level of scrutiny for the for-profit sector. Whether for-profit institutions receive more or less scrutiny at the state level than fifteen or twenty years ago is uncertain. And whether they should receive more or less scrutiny will continue to be a public policy question for the foreseeable future.

Federal Oversight

The federal government became involved in the regulation of the for-profit sector after its decision to include for-profit institutions as eligible destinations for GI bill beneficiaries in the 1940s. Initially relying on state judgments of quality, the 1952 reauthorization of the GI bill established the importance of accreditation as a marker of educational legitimacy. For-profit institutions that wanted access to federal funds had to succumb not just to state authorization that legally enabled them to operate as educational institutions but also to the external peer review procedures established by accrediting agencies. As early as the 1960s, for-profit schools had become a "semi-public business" (Miller and Hamilton, 1964, p. 151), with the price of entry defined by the rules and restrictions established by accreditors and regulators. As education has not traditionally been a federal responsibility, the national government used the power of the purse to compel states and accreditors to shape the system they desired.

Participation of for-profit higher education in federal aid programs was relatively modest until 1972, when the sector was explicitly included in the reauthorization of the Higher Education Act on essentially equal footing with not-for-profit private and public sector institutions. More than any other action, this parity brought for-profit higher education into the universe of postsecondary education in the United States and gave it a legal and financial stature unique to its history (Trivett, 1974). The federal government did not use this occasion to identify for-profit institutions as needing special regulation distinct from any other postsecondary institution. Rather, the first attempt at federal regulation directed toward the for-profit sector involved fraud and abuse allegations in which the FTC took the lead (Lee and Merisotis, 1990). Extensive hearings were held on the issue, and in 1973, a consumer protection campaign against for-profit correspondence schools was initiated based on the institutions' low completion rates, aggressive advertising, and high loan default rates (Trivett, 1974). The FTC published a catalog of deceptive practices and clamped down on correspondence schools. Many went out of business in the face of increased scrutiny of their business methods (Merwin, 1981). The U.S. Office of Education picked up on the issue and published a taxonomy of abusive practices, determining that proprietary schools had a higher potential for abuse than not-for-profit private and public institutions (Jung, 1980).

Based on this evidence and the findings of their own investigations, the FTC became interested in regulating the entire proprietary school industry.

In 1978, the agency proposed a rule that would have forced the for-profit sector to provide graduation and employment rates, establish standard tuition reimbursement policies, and give students the right to cancel enrollment contracts (Lee and Merisotis, 1990; Lipinsky de Orlov, 1981). For-profit schools sued to prevent the rule from taking place, arguing that the broad brush of the regulation unfairly targeted all institutions for the transgressions of the few (Lee and Merisotis, 1990). The court actually upheld several of the specific requirements in the rule, including the publication of graduation rates and the contract cancellation provision. The rule as a whole, however, was rejected primarily because the FTC defined unfair practices as violations of the rules to prevent unfair practices (Lipinsky de Orlov, 1981). This circularity of argument doomed the FTC's attempt, and the court ordered the rule to be rewritten, effectively canceling implementation of any regulatory requirement. The agency attempted several times in the 1980s to revive the rule but ultimately was unsuccessful in establishing the broad regulatory authority over the for-profit sector it had sought (Lee and Merisotis, 1990).

The U.S. Department of Education again took up the issue in the late 1980s, following up on its predecessor Office of Education study of the for-profit sector a decade earlier. In a series of reports (for example, Fitzgerald and Harmon, 1988; Schenet, 1990), the department found that the regulatory structure for the for-profit sector was weak and unable to address the significant problems endemic to these institutions.[26] Questionable practices regarding recruitment and admissions echoed the findings of the earlier study. Further, additional problems were identified in the sector, including awarding aid to ineligible students and high dropout and loan default rates. The rules put into place to address the problems identified in the 1970s applied equally to all institutions. Now regulations were considered that would single out for-profit institutions for special scrutiny. The primary result was the so-called 85–15 rule, which required a for-profit institution to derive at least 15 percent of its revenues from sources other than federal student aid programs. In essence, this rule forced a minimal level of nonsubsidized support for the educational programs offered by for-profit institutions. Several other rules were implemented that, although they applied to all institutions equally, disproportionately affected the for-profit sector. The 50 percent rule declared ineligible institutions that offered more than half their programs off campus. The twelve-hour rule required full-time students to have the equivalent of twelve hours per week of instructional "seat time." Commission payments to admission representatives were prohibited. Limitations on branch campuses were put in place. And maximum default rates of 25 percent were established, preventing participation in student loan programs for those institutions that violated the limit for three consecutive years.

The combined effect of these rules was dramatic. The number of for-profit institutions declined sharply, with closures and bankruptcies particularly evident in low-income inner cities and among large corporate chains (Moore, 1995). Borrowing rates declined for students in less-than-four-year for-profit institutions (Wei, Li, and Berkner, 2004), and overall default rates in the for-profit sector declined from more than 30 percent to less than 10 percent (*The College Access and Opportunity Act: Are Students at Proprietary Institutions Treated Equitably Under Current Law?*, 2004). What was perceived as a for-profit sector run amok was effectively corralled by regulations tied to eligibility for student loans. Ironically for institutions that had prided themselves on their market sensibility and independence, a substantial reliance on federal aid money exposed them to the regulatory authority they had avoided for so many years.

In addition to the FTC and the U.S. Department of Education, SEC represents another significant source of regulation for the for-profit sector. Its authority, however, extends only to those for-profit institutions that are owned by a publicly traded corporation. Nevertheless, these shareholder institutions have kept the agency busy. Since the 1980s, SEC investigations have been a regular feature of the for-profit education industry. Most often the focus has been on misleading statements to investors regarding enrollment or financial viability of expansion plans, which have occasionally presaged the downfall of the corporation (the dissolution of NEC described earlier is perhaps the best example).

SEC has investigated several of the current publicly owned education corporations. Beginning in 2003, Career Education Corporation was faced with several accusations of misrepresentation and inflation of stock values, triggering investigations by the SEC. A question was raised in 2004 about how the

Apollo Group represented to shareholders the material nature of a Department of Education inquiry into the University of Phoenix. Also in 2004, Corinthian Colleges was investigated based on allegations by shareholders that they were misled about the financial status of the company. At the same time, ITT Educational Services caught the attention of investigators for allegedly falsifying records on grades and attendance (Sachdev, 2004; "Shareholder Suit Hits Apollo," 2004).

The power of SEC is fairly substantial, and even news that the agency is considering an investigation can materially affect a corporation's finances. But despite the spate of inquiries since 2003, no real effort has been made to investigate the for-profit education sector as an industry. SEC has not singled out the for-profit sector for any special regulation, and most of the recent inquiries have been closed with no findings of wrongdoing. SEC has an indirect impact on the for-profit sector, though it may be seen as a double-edged sword. On the one hand, because public companies must make quarterly filings to the SEC and because those reports are scrutinized widely by investors who demand continuous growth to justify elevated stock prices, the companies are under pressure to accentuate the positive elements of their operations while downplaying negative aspects of the corporate strategy. The SEC's regulatory authority presents a strong barrier against crossing the line from corporate promotion to misleading and fraudulent statements that have historically plagued the sector. On the other hand, the filings required by the agency may also be seen as a driver of profit at the expense of educational quality. The enormous growth of the for-profit sector since the mid-1990s has been marked by the need for publicly owned for-profit educational corporations to meet quarterly financial targets. Because SEC is charged with protecting investors' interests in the market, the sector is largely measured in terms of its profitability and market penetration rather than its educational contributions to the postsecondary system. In other words, SEC regulatory authority does little to ensure that students or society are getting their money's worth. Still, because of the size and scope of shareholder institutions, SEC will likely become a significant player in the regulation of the sector over the next decade.

Other federal agencies have some oversight over the for-profit sector: the U.S. Department of Veterans Affairs approves institutions for certain programs sponsored by the government for former members of the military, and the Federal Aviation Administration licenses aviation schools. And private citizens have regularly used the federal False Claims Act since 1986 to sue for-profit institutions for violations of federal law (Davis, 1994). The False Claims Act allows anyone with direct knowledge of a violation of federal law the right to initiate legal proceedings in the place of the federal government and receive a portion of any resulting fine. Violations of federal aid policies are often the subject of these claims. Suits filed under this act may actually exert a substantial regulatory pressure on the for-profit sector, even though formal federal action is not required to settle the case.

Diploma Mills

Diploma mills are fraudulent institutions that exist on the margins of the regulatory framework in the United States. They do not have recognized accreditation, nor do they participate in federal aid programs under the U.S. Department of Education. Diploma mills are not publicly traded corporations, so the SEC's reporting requirements do not apply. The absence of an external regulatory authority, however, does not necessarily identify an institution as a diploma mill. Certain states and countries with rather lax policies for recognizing educational institutions give a patina of legitimacy to some institutions under a regulatory framework defined by the lack of regulation. Accreditation and participation in federal aid programs are not requirements for operation as an educational institution. The market in educational credentials does not need the imprimatur of Wall Street. And a whole range of institutions, from religious schools to technical certification enterprises, offer valid credentials without adopting the traditional markers of educational legitimacy. Diploma mills are different from these other providers in that they are profit-making entities in the business of awarding academic credentials requiring little or no academic work. The activities of diploma mills are generally illegal, though establishing jurisdiction for enforcement purposes is often difficult. In its role as a consumer protection agency, the FTC has emerged as the leading federal body concerned with their proliferation. Among the states, Oregon serves as a clearinghouse for information about diploma mills.

The major effort of both state and federal governments is to distinguish diploma mills from their legitimate cousins offering valid—though nontraditional—educational services. In an echo of its efforts in the 1970s against correspondence schools, the FTC has teamed up with the U.S. Department of Education in a campaign to inform consumers of the telltale signs of a diploma mill (Federal Trade Commission, 2005a, 2005b). The FTC warns of institutions that claim accreditation from an agency not approved by the U.S. Department of Education, have sound-alike names, and require no attendance or offer degrees for flat fees. The campaign also urges employers to verify applicants' academic credentials and to look for quickie degrees and degrees awarded from schools in different locations from where the applicant lives and works. The Oregon Office of Degree Authorization (2005) publishes a list of institutions that it has not been able to verify as legitimate providers of postsecondary education. Widely noted as the publisher of an authoritative guide to diploma mills currently operating in the United States, Oregon relies primarily on the accreditation status of the institution to identify illegitimate institutions and suggests that unaccredited institutions based in Alabama, California, Hawaii, Idaho, Mississippi, Montana, and Wyoming should be viewed with suspicion, regardless of their state approval. These states have a reputation for hosting diploma mills because of weak state regulations or poor enforcement of existing regulations.[27] Both the FTC and the state of Oregon base their efforts on eliminating the market for bogus degrees by drawing attention to how they operate and emphasizing the responsibility of employers to reject applicants who present fraudulent credentials.

A third front in the battle against diploma mills is the U.S. Congress. Although the general topic of for-profit higher education has been regularly addressed on Capitol Hill, the sector as a whole rather than the specific attributes of diploma mills has been the subject. In 2002, however, hearings on these institutions began in the U.S. Senate. In an elegant strategy designed to highlight the lack of educational standards at diploma mills, Senator Susan Collins of Maine obtained several degrees from a nonexistent "Lexington University" simply by paying a fee (Cramer, 2002). Additional hearings pointed out how the federal government has been lax in enforcing its own restrictions against its employees' using degrees from diploma mills (Cramer, 2004). More than one thousand individuals on the federal payroll, including twenty-eight senior employees, were found to hold degrees from institutions identified as diploma mills. As is the case with the work of the FTC and the state of Oregon, the dual strategy employed by Senator Collins against diploma mills is to expose their activities and to institute policies to reduce or eliminate the market for false educational credentials.

Current Regulatory Issues

Two main issues currently relate to the regulation of the for-profit sector. The first relates to the continuing challenge of dealing with diploma mills, cross-state institutions, and distance education institutions. The second involves the reauthorization of the federal Higher Education Act.

Diploma mills and cross-state and distance education institutions represent distinct dilemmas for regulators, and while the issues overlap, they do not have a common solution. Diploma mills, for example, often move from state to state and offer ersatz distance education. Regulation formerly focused on out-of-state degrees and restrictions on distance education as a way of tackling these institutions. Recently, however, legitimate multistate and online institutions have become commonplace, and rules limiting their operation are falling aside. Nevertheless, as the investigations by the FTC, the U.S. Congress, and the state of Oregon have made clear, controlling diploma mills requires tightening state laws to better distinguish these institutions from their legitimate cousins, and it requires the public exposure and consistent prosecution of fraudulent business practices under existing regulation. The growth of multistate institutions suggests that existing state-specific regulations will become more difficult to defend. The University of Phoenix, for example, has effectively demolished state borders as a relevant barrier to the expansion of higher education, and the institution can now point to successful operations across the country as it continues its inevitable conquest of the remaining holdout states. Finally, the triumph of distance education has been not in the for-profit sector but among public colleges and universities. Its ubiquity there suggests that public policy will continue to embrace online and virtual universities and reduce the for-profit connection with low quality and hucksterism that has marked the field from correspondence schools to the early Internet colleges.

Although the issues related to regulating for-profit distance education and multistate institutions and to the problems posed by diploma mills are important, they are mostly being addressed piecemeal. The accreditation community and individual states are individually tackling the issues, and with the exception of the FTC campaign and Senator Collins's investigation of diploma mills, the national regulatory role in these matters is limited. The situation changes dramatically with the reauthorization of the HEA, however. This piece of legislation has engendered much discussion, lobbying, and outright arm-twisting, with the for-profit sector playing a fairly significant role in the debate over its passage (*The College Access and Opportunity Act: Are Students at Proprietary Institutions Treated Equitably Under Current Law?*, 2004; Kinser, 2004a). Because the federal aid provisions of Title IV represent a significant source of funding for for-profit higher education, representatives of the sector are eager to revise the legislation to extend institutional eligibility for additional aid and remove restrictions that limit their ability to participate fully in federal programs (Career College Association, 2004).[28]

The issues at play go back to the regulations established in the late 1980s and early 1990s to address the perceptions of widespread fraud and abuse by for-profit institutions participating in the federal student aid programs. These regulatory actions were so successful at reducing problems in the sector that advocates of revision now suggest that the reforms are no longer needed. Moreover, the for-profit sector is seeking to be treated just as any other postsecondary institution under the regulations, rejecting the targeted policies and requirements based on old assumptions of the for-profits' malfeasance. Minor debates on these matters surround the accelerated degree and distance education provisions inserted into the HEA in 1992 (the 50 percent and the twelve-hour rules), but the big disputes are focused on two provisions in the act that specifically target the for-profit sector.

The first dispute relates to the for-profit sector's traditional concern to be treated equally as eligible institutions for the disbursement of student aid

(Petrello, 1987). The provision is the so-called 90–10 rule—a for-profit institution can receive no more than 90 percent of its revenue from federal student aid programs—which was modified in 1998 from its original 85–15 proportions. Proponents of the for-profit sector argue that this provision hurts their ability to serve low-income students; those in favor of the provision counter that the ratio represents a minimal burden and ensures that institutions will not exist simply to collect federal monies (Kinser, 2004a). The second dispute involves how the HEA defines postsecondary institutions. The for-profit sector argues that a single definition should include all eligible institutions instead of the two-pronged version that treats for-profit institutions separately. Those opposed to a single definition point out that for-profit institutions are already eligible for student aid under the current definitions; implementing a single definition would make for-profit institutions themselves eligible for aid and other benefits that go beyond the scope of appropriate public support for a profit-making entity (Kinser, 2004a).

That these issues are facing the for-profit sector now is a rather interesting development. Since the first federal aid to students was proposed, for-profit institutions have consistently argued for their fair share in the interest of serving students. At the same time, the sector has historically disclaimed its interest in becoming another government-sponsored sector and has rejected past suggestions that they wished to gain access to institutional aid. Jones (1973), for example, states that the "declared philosophy" of the for-profit sector is to ensure that their students are eligible for aid. "These schools have never asked," he continues, "and in my opinion will never ask, for any type of institutional aid" (p. 180). The structure of the HEA as established in 1972 adopted the for-profit philosophy and made student aid widely available while restricting institutional and other aid to the public and private not-for-profit sectors. The emergence of an expanded degree-granting for-profit sector has apparently christened a new philosophy, one that is based on regulatory equivalency rather than distinctiveness.

Reflections and Future Direction

THE HISTORY OF FOR-PROFIT HIGHER EDUCATION in the United States does not represent a simple trajectory. Growth and expansion have regularly been followed by decline and contraction. In the current Wall Street era, the fortunes of the sector are ascendant. Double-digit growth and a transformation to degree-granting status mark the certain rise of for-profit higher education in recent years. The higher education community of the future looks to reject the public-private dichotomy that has held for so long and to embrace the for-profit sector as one of its own. But there is nothing inevitable about this narrative. In the midst of a trend, it is important to look for the countervailing forces that suggest that the pendulum is swinging. At the same time, one should not engage in wishful reminiscence of a golden age, where pure institutions offered learning for its own sake and students desired only to develop a meaningful philosophy of life. It is a revisionist historian who suggests that time ever existed and a quixotic venture to see it recaptured. For-profit higher education has proved to be a resilient organizational form, weathering the development of public subsidies and scrutiny, regulation and reform. It will not simply go away, no matter the scandals and improprieties that regularly remind one of the sector's attractiveness to scoundrels. Looking to the future, then, the question is whether the for-profit sector will remain marginal or grow to become a mainstay of the higher education enterprise.

Since the 1940s, for-profit higher education has cycled between achievement and notoriety. GI bill participation in the training of veterans turned to regulation of fraudulent behavior in the 1950s. The promise of accreditation and full participation in federal student aid programs opened the sector to criticisms of low standards and weak outcomes in the 1970s. The heady days of national expansion and market capitalization in the 1980s were the foundation for a 1990s backlash that closed egregious student loan violators and tightened control over the sector as a whole. The rebound seen today began in the mid-1990s, and, true to form, a spate of investigations a decade later threatens to dampen enthusiasm for the new shareholder institutions and their corporate owners. The confident prognosticator sits back and waits for the pendulum to swing, returning the for-profit sector to its former existence serving the margins of postsecondary education.

This scenario might occur for several reasons. Enrollment growth, though phenomenal, has been concentrated among four-year schools and has been dominated by the increases represented by the University of Phoenix. Such rates cannot be sustained in a mature higher education environment, and the possibility of other national shareholder universities emerging to duplicate the Phoenix model seems remote (Breneman, 2005). Moreover, the size of the for-profit sector remains small in comparison with the not-for-profit private and public sectors. Though they represent about one-fifth of all institutions, most have enrollments under five hundred students. In fact, only eleven for-profit campuses have enrollments greater than five thousand students, and four of them offer nearly all their instruction online (National Center for Education Statistics, 2004a).[29] The public and private not-for-profit sectors added more than 600,000 students between 2001 and 2002, nearly 20,000 more students than were enrolled in all degree-granting for-profit institutions combined (National Center for Education Statistics, 2004b, 2005). Expansion of degree-granting for-profit institutions notwithstanding, the sector awards fewer than 5 percent of the degrees in the United States, the majority of which are associate degrees. It awards just 2 percent of the bachelor's degrees, 3 percent of the master's, and fewer than 2 percent of doctorates (National Center for Education Statistics, 2003b). Among degree-granting institutions, the for-profit sector represents slightly more than a rounding error in U.S. higher education. Any one of the big shareholder universities could collapse and drop the numbers to insignificance—the rise and fall of the NEC in the 1980s is an object lesson to those who react with skepticism at this thought. From historic as well as contemporary perspectives, then, today's large for-profit institutions and their giant corporate sponsors are an anomaly. The pendulum swings.

Other elements are at play, however, that suggest the Wall Street era may represent a fundamental shift in the organization of the for-profit sector. The capital available for expansion by publicly owned corporations is substantial, and the number of small, independent for-profit institutions is large. Nearly 70 percent of degree-granting for-profit institutions with enrollments greater than one thousand are publicly owned, compared with about 28 percent of those with fewer than one thousand students, representing a huge potential market for expansion by acquisition. The student market in the United States may not be saturated either, as some evidence suggests that much of the for-profit enrollment comes from students who are not well served by traditional institutions (Breneman, 2005; Kelly, 2001). Sufficient numbers of high school graduates and adults who have not attended college can fuel the growth of degree-granting for-profit higher education for the foreseeable future. The major for-profit institutions have achieved name-brand status and a substantial alumni base that creates additional value and may translate into tangible goodwill in ongoing policy debates. Looking beyond the United States, globalization and privatization have opened the door to cross-border providers of education, and corporations are beginning to look overseas to satisfy their needs for expansion (Kinser and Levy, 2005). Higher education itself has changed as well, with job training and workforce development becoming the personal and public policy goals of attending college. Fewer students are studying the liberal arts while career-oriented disciplines enjoy record growth. Part-time and contingent faculty are increasingly the norm. The claim that colleges and universities should be for the public good is on the defensive. Private sector priorities are embedded in global discussions about improving access to higher education. In all of these examples, the for-profit sector matches the spirit of the times.

Research Agenda

The transformation of for-profit higher education has made the assumptions of past eras problematic when applied to the sector today. Changes in faculty roles, curricular models, and academic decision making over the last half century have questionable relevance to the corporate-owned campuses of the Wall Street era. Student enrollment patterns have certainly changed over time, yet beyond counting who matriculates where, nearly the entire realm of the student experience in today's for-profit sector is based on historical surveys. The regulation and accreditation of for-profit higher education are substantially different now than in decades past, but the impact of various state and accreditation policies on the sector has not been substantially updated. And it is not just the latest era that needs attention. The history of for-profit higher education has not been reviewed in forty years, and much remains to be learned from an all-but-forgotten archive of information on the sector that has accumulated for more than a century.

Areas needing further investigation have been noted throughout this volume. This section proposes five broad topics to focus attention on major gaps of knowledge about the for-profit sector.

1. *A descriptive profile of for-profit higher education.* Although basic, a descriptive profile of the for-profit sector is needed to ground all the other analyses. It is a significant hindrance to not know how pervasive certain features of the sector are or whether large segments of the sector are unaccounted for. Clear classifications of for-profit institutions need to be established to avoid gross generalizations based on limited understanding of the inherent diversity of the sector. Distortions inserted into analyses because of the overwhelming presence of a few large institutions need to be documented.

2. *For-profit academic models.* The efficacy of various academic models employed by the for-profit sector need to be established, including degree- and non-degree-granting institutions and curricula. Consideration should be given to economic efficiency as well as to efficient mastery of knowledge. An element of this investigation must also be a more complete understanding of faculty role. In particular, a better accounting is needed of how practical knowledge is developed in the classroom in concert or in conflict with academic and theoretical knowledge.

3. *Student experiences.* So little is known about what students experience as the central participants in for-profit higher education that one hesitates to suggest primary targets for investigation. Two areas of students'

experiences, however, would be quite helpful in understanding the sector and anticipating its future. The first is determining how and why students choose a for-profit institution, particularly compared with the not-for-profit private and public institutions. The second is determining the range of developmental, academic, and economic outcomes associated with a for-profit education.

4. *International expansion.* In much of the world, traditions of private higher education are rather weak, and the for-profit sector exists in murky legal territory (Kinser and Levy, 2005). The growth of for-profit higher education globally, particularly by multinational corporations, is a new phenomenon that is augmented by revisions to trade agreements and the siren song of privatization's impacting all government services. The interest among corporations from the United States and other developed countries in the international market is clear. What is less clear is how cross-border educational arrangements are made, their legal and regulatory status, and the extent of local participation in developing educational opportunities.

5. *History of for-profit higher education.* No comprehensive account of the history of for-profit higher education has been attempted since the 1960s. Both a broad history of the sector from its beginnings and a more concentrated focus on the transformations since the 1970s are warranted.

For-profit higher education may be seen as a distinctive institutional type in each of these areas, but it should also be considered alongside traditional not-for-profit private and public institutions as part of the larger higher education enterprise. For example, the for-profit sector is rarely mentioned in existing histories and is never presented as a significant participant in the developing educational character of the United States. An account that weaves the for-profit sector into a more complex narrative of the modern system of higher education would be a valuable addition to the historical literature. Similarly, a universal theory of college choice should consider the for-profit sector, along with other nontraditional options, as one of the legitimate alternatives for postsecondary study available to students. Much can be learned about the for-profit sector and its relationship to the rest of higher education, even when research questions are segregated to provide sector-specific answers.

Conclusion

A future scholar may look back on the Wall Street era and wonder what all the fuss was about. Sectoral labels will have blurred by then, and the angst with which writers considered the implications of the for-profit model, the decline in government support for public institutions, or the fiscal pressures threatening the survival of the private liberal arts college will seem quaint. Just as a current observer concerned with teaching career-oriented students today may read the Yale Report of 1828 and consider its emphasis on the furniture and discipline of the mind to be rather beside the point, an insistence on labeling all institutions based on an anachronistic funding model may have little to do with what the future of higher education will bring. The system will have evolved, much as it always has, to meet societal needs and market demands.

On the other hand, the future scholar may see in this era a watershed moment in the history of higher education. Here, in the Wall Street era, awareness of for-profit higher education is not matched with adequate understanding of its implications, even as the decisions being made today open the door to dramatic changes and unforeseen consequences. These changes may be for the best—Harvard, Johns Hopkins, and Wisconsin joined with Phoenix as universities that made a difference in American higher education—or they may represent real loss if the distinctive role of the academy in society is reduced. The for-profit sector may continue to grow to become a coequal branch of the higher education enterprise, providing a teaching-oriented focus that is lacking in so many not-for-profit private and public institutions (Breneman, 2005). Or as the acceptance of market values in place of academic values reaches a tipping point (Kezar, Chambers, and Burkhardt, 2005), the for-profit sector may become emblematic of the attack on higher education for the public good.

The last volume in the ASHE report series to concentrate on for-profit higher education concluded with a plea for "all parties with a stake in the debate about proprietary schools [to] initiate better research" (Lee and Merisotis, 1990, p. 80). It is disappointing to have to repeat this call fifteen years later and, along with the authors noted in the opening chapter, add to the long series of appeals for better information about these institutions, their owners, and their activities. The for-profit sector is currently playing an outsized role in the ongoing transformation of higher education. It is imperative that its growing influence is understood, not through the shrill opinions and arguments of true believers and cynical backbenchers but through the careful analysis of trends, the application of theory, and the reasonable interpretation of a substantive body of research.

Notes

1. Financial analysts presumably know quite a bit about for-profit institutions (see, for example, Ortmann, 2001), but their assessments are limited to the economics of the sector.

2. Globally, the phrase "third sector" generally refers to private nonprofit institutions. In the United States and other countries with well-established nonprofit private higher education institutions, however, for-profit higher education shows much parallel with the emergence of new private institutions in systems traditionally dominated by public sector institutions (Kinser and Levy, 2005).

3. Until the mid-1990s, NCES defined a proprietary institution as one that is "under private control but whose profits derive from revenues subject to taxation" (National Center for Education Statistics, 1991).

4. It is noteworthy that some forms of for-profit higher education became well established during this period, including correspondence schools and trade schools, while proprietary medical schools declined and essentially disappeared. The reasons for these differential outcomes in the early twentieth century beg for in-depth historical analysis.

5. Except where noted, company information on the twelve corporations discussed in this chapter is drawn from corporate annual reports and other SEC filings, *PR Newswire* reports accessed through the Lexis-Nexis database, and the *International Directory of Company Histories,* various years and volumes, published by St. James Press (*International Directory of Company Histories,* 1988–2004). In addition to the twelve corporations discussed here, two other corporations filed for initial public offerings in 2005: Capella University and Lincoln Educational Services Corporation. Corporations that own limited numbers of for-profit institutions through a subsidiary are not addressed in this discussion. For example, Thomson owns Education Direct, a degree-granting correspondence school.

6. All prices of initial public offerings (IPOs) are based on the company's prospectus or contemporary press accounts of the sale. Because of later stock splits and additional offerings, they are generally not directly comparable with current stock prices. Other financial information, unless otherwise noted, is based on values as of January 2005.

7. A tracking stock allows investors to buy a portion of a corporation's business without requiring the parent company to spin off the division as an independent company. Issuing tracking stocks for Internet-related operations of larger companies was a frequent tactic in the late 1990s. As the dot-com boom faded, however, most of them were reabsorbed into the parent company (Krantz, 2004).

8. Phillips Colleges was a private company that quickly expanded in the 1980s, owning more than eighty-five schools at its peak in 1989 before its scandal-driven decline in the 1990s.

9. Larson was a Vice President at NEC from 1980–1989, during the company's profitable expansion period. He left just before the CEO was forced out in 1990 amid shareholder lawsuits and corporate financial trouble. Lawson's tenure at Phillips Colleges lasted from 1989 to 1993, when that company

was caught up in a series of investigations for illegal recruitment practices and student loan violation. Phillips started selling schools to remain afloat, ultimately leaving the education field in 1996 when it sold its remaining campuses to Corinthian Colleges.

10. Distance education programs are generally prohibited from participating in Title IV financial aid programs. The distance education demonstration program was established through the 1998 amendments to the Higher Education Act as an experiment in expanding access to a limited number of these institutions. Of the twenty-nine institutions currently participating, nine are for-profit institutions and five are shareholder institutions (owned by Apollo, Kaplan, CEC, and Laureate) (U.S. Department of Education, 2005).

11. A similar point can be made about the influence of investors in privately held Venture institutions.

12. Data on the for-profit sector from HEGIS are available from the late 1960s, but enrollment figures have not been published for years before 1976.

13. Current data are lacking on this point. The most recent published information on the curriculum at non-degree-granting institutions is by Apling (1993).

14. Although investment analysts' calculations regarding the potential demand for a for-profit education frequently assume a beneficial relationship, they seem to reflect market assumptions rather than "privileged knowledge" regarding outcomes (Ortmann, 2001).

15. Many for-profit institutions offer accelerated bachelor's degree programs, presumably to meet students needs. There is no graduation rate information that compares how students do in accelerated programs with their success in regular term programs.

16. Institutions of higher education are defined as institutions offering "college level studies" creditable toward a degree (National Center for Education Statistics, 1991, p. 441).

17. Based on calculations using faculty data from the 2002 Apollo Group 12 annual report. Citing the University of Phoenix as his source, Breneman (forthcoming) provides numbers for faculty employed by Phoenix in 2002 that are about one-third lower than what is given in the Apollo Group report for that year. Considering corporate obligations for accurate filings, the figure from the annual report is likely more reliable.

18. Other accounts contradict this assertion, finding that for-profit faculty do a significant amount of work for the money they are paid (Kelly, 2001; Kinser, 2005b).

19. It is often noted that the University of Phoenix regularly assesses student learning (Berg, 2005), but these data are for internal use and have not been independently analyzed.

20. Petrello (1987, p. 82) quotes a resolution from the North Central Association in 1923 that recognized "Private Commercial Schools" as eligible institutions.

21. Erwin (1975) reports that 63.1 percent of all for-profit institutions are accredited or approved by a federal agency for financial aid funds. It is likely that fewer than half the institutions he counts in that figure are actually accredited.

22. According to the ACCSCT (2003, p. 2), for example, "A school must describe and disclose itself consistently to each accrediting agency, state agency, and federal agency with regard to identity (i.e., main school, branch, or equivalent), purpose, governance, programs, credentials awarded, personnel, finances, and constituents served, and must keep each agency apprised of any change in its status."

23. The U.S. General Accounting Office prepared a Senate report in 1990 on the activities of seven national agencies that accredit for-profit institutions but did not specifically address their standards for accreditation (Frazier, 1990).

24. It is likely, however, that some states did take an active interest in the for-profit sector during the nineteenth century. Duff's Business Institute (2005), for example, claims that it received a charter from Pennsylvania authorities in 1851 that enabled it to operate as the first business college in the United States. Additionally, prominent politicians participated in for-profit business college conventions in the 1860s (Knepper, 1941).

25. All states have consumer protection laws that apply to deceptive sales of goods and services. They do apply to proprietary schools, although such a complaint-driven system is not a substitute for formal regulation (Schenet, 1990, p. 15).

26. For a full list of reports generated in this investigation, see the bibliography prepared by Salinas and Monagle (1991).

27. The basis for this reputation deserves closer attention. In Wyoming, for example, the state has been trying to close a large loophole for religious institutions (Gruver, 2005).

28. The Career College Association lobbied extensively on reauthorizing the Higher Education Act, promoting such initiatives as eliminating barriers to transferring credits between regionally and nationally accredited institutions, revising non-sector-specific accountability measures, and revising rules that call for additional scrutiny of institutions when they change ownership. The federal aid issues, however, reflect the sector's fundamental concerns (Career College Association, 2004; Kinser, 2004a).

29. The online campuses are Capella University, Kaplan College, the University of Phoenix Online, and Walden University. The other seven campuses are Academy of Art College, American Intercontinental University–Atlanta, three DeVry campuses, and two additional University of Phoenix campuses. All except Academy of Art College are—or in the case of Capella, soon will be—publicly traded shareholder institutions.

References

Accrediting Commission of Career Schools and Colleges of Technology. (2002). *Annual report and performance indicators.* Arlington, VA: Accrediting Commission of Career Schools and Colleges of Technology.

Accrediting Commission of Career Schools and Colleges of Technology. (2003). *Standards of accreditation.* Arlington, VA: Accrediting Commission of Career Schools and Colleges of Technology.

Accrediting Council for Independent Colleges and Schools. (2004). *2003–2004 annual report.* Washington, DC: Accrediting Council for Independent Colleges and Schools.

Adelman, C. (2000). *A parallel postsecondary universe: The certification system in information technology.* Washington, DC: Office of Educational Research and Improvement, U.S. Department of Education. (ED 445 246)

Allen, I. E., and Seaman, J. (2004). *Entering the mainstream: The quality and extent of online education in the United States, 2003 and 2004.* Needham & Wellesley, MA: Sloan Consortium.

Alstete, J. W. (2004). *Accreditation matters: Achieving academic recognition and renewal.* ASHE Higher Education Report (vol. 30, no. 4). San Francisco: Jossey-Bass.

Altbach, P. G. (2001, Fall). The rise of the pseudouniversity. *International Higher Education, 25,* 2–3.

American Association of Cosmetology Schools. (2005). *AACS membership.* Retrieved March 31, 2005, from http://www.beautyschools.org.

American Colleges of Hairstyling. (2000). *Barber school history.* Retrieved December 3, 2004, from http://www.americancollegeofhair.com/history.html.

Apling, R. N. (1993). Proprietary schools and their students. *Journal of Higher Education, 64*(4), 379–416.

Apollo Group. (2002). *Annual report.* Phoenix, AZ: Apollo Group, Inc.

Apollo Group. (2004). *Annual report.* Phoenix, AZ: Apollo Group, Inc.

Bailey, T. R. (2003). A researcher's perspective. In A. C. McCormick and R. D. Cox (Eds.), *Classification systems for two-year colleges* (pp. 93–100). San Francisco: Jossey-Bass.

Bailey, T. R., Badway, N., and Gumport, P. J. (2003). *For-profit higher education and community colleges.* Stanford, CA: Stanford University, National Center for Postsecondary Improvement.

Barker, A. (2004, February 19). Internet college makes gains toward accreditation. *Charleston [West Virginia] Daily Press.*

Bartlett, T. (2005, March 11). Education company buys religious college. *Chronicle of Higher Education,* A31.

Belitsky, A. H. (1969). *Private vocational schools and their students: Limited objectives, unlimited opportunities.* Cambridge, MA: Schenkman Publishing Company.

Berg, G. A. (2005). *Lessons from the edge: For-profit and nontraditional higher education in America.* Westport, CT: Praeger Publishers.

Blumenstyk, G. (2004, May 14). For-profit colleges face new scrutiny. *Chronicle of Higher Education,* A1.

Bok, D. (2003). *Universities in the marketplace: The commercialization of higher education.* Princeton, NJ: Princeton University Press.

Bolino, A. C. (1973). *Career education: Contributions to economic growth.* New York: Praeger Publishers.

Bollag, B. (2004, September 3). For the love of God (and money). *Chronicle of Higher Education,* A29.

Breneman, D. (2005). Entrepreneurship in higher education. In B. Pusser (Ed.), *Arenas of entrepreneurship: Where nonprofit and for-profit institutions compete* (pp. 3–10). San Francisco: Jossey-Bass.

Breneman, D. (Forthcoming). The University of Phoenix: Icon of for-profit higher education. In D. Breneman (Ed.), *Earnings from learning: The rise of for-profit universities.* Albany, NY: State University of New York Press.

Brimah, T. (2000). *Survey analysis: State statutes and regulations governing the operation of degree-granting for-profit institutions of higher education* (State notes: For-profit/proprietary). Denver: Education Commission of the States.

Burd, S. (2004, July 30). Selling out higher education policy? *Chronicle of Higher Education,* A16–A19.

Byce, C., and Schmitt, C. M. (1992). *Students at less-than-four-year institutions: Contractor report* (NCES 92–206). Washington, DC: Office of Educational Research and Improvement, U.S. Department of Education.

Cahalan, M., Roey, S., Fernandez, R., and Barbett, S. (1996). *Fall staff in postsecondary institutions, 1993* (NCES 96–323). Washington, DC: National Center for Education Statistics, U.S. Department of Education.

Career College Association. (2004). *Annual report: 2003–2004.* Washington, DC: Career College Association.

Carnegie Foundation for the Advancement of Teaching. (1987, January/February). Career schools: An overview. *Change,* 21–34.

Center for Policy Analysis. (2004). *Choice of institution: Changing student attendance patterns in the 1990s* (ACE Issue Brief). Washington, DC: American Council on Education.

Chaloux, B. N. (1985, April 19). *State oversight of the private and proprietary sector.* Paper presented at a meeting of the National Association of Trade and Technical Schools and the Association of Independent Colleges and Schools, Miami, FL.

Cheng, X. D., and Levin, B. H. (1995). Who are the students at community colleges and proprietary schools? In D. A. Clowes and E. M. Hawthorne (Eds.), *Community colleges and proprietary schools: Conflict or convergence?* (pp. 51–60). San Francisco: Jossey-Bass.

Chronicle of Higher Education. (2004, November 5). The Chronicle index of for-profit higher education. *Chronicle of Higher Education,* A28.

Chung, A. (2004, November 4). *Who are the proprietary students? An analysis of NPSAS 1996 and NPSAS 2000.* Paper presented at a meeting of the Association for the Study of Higher Education, Kansas City, MO.

Clark, H. F., and Sloan, H. S. (1966). *Classrooms on Main Street: An account of specialty schools in the United States that train for work and leisure.* New York: Teachers College Press.

Clowes, D. A., and Hawthorne, E. M. (Eds.). (1995). *Community colleges and proprietary schools: Conflict or convergence?* (Vol. 91). San Francisco: Jossey-Bass.

The college access and opportunity act: Are students at proprietary institutions treated equitably under current law? (2004). Hearing before the U.S. House of Representatives, 108th Congress, 2nd Session [Serial No. 108–63].

Commission on Colleges. (2001). *Principles of accreditation: Foundations for quality enhancement.* Decatur, GA: Southern Association of Schools and Colleges.

Cooperative Institutional Research Program. (2004). *Institutions participating in the CIRP freshman survey program, 1966–2004.* Los Angeles: Higher Education Research Institute, University of California, Los Angeles.

Coughlin, E. (1977, April 4). Bar association suspends policy against accrediting proprietary law schools. *Chronicle of Higher Education.*

Council on Occupational Education. (2004). *Handbook of accreditation: 2004 edition.* Atlanta: Council on Occupational Education.

Cramer, R. J. (2002). *Purchases of degrees from diploma mills* (GAO-03–269R). Washington, DC: U.S. General Accounting Office.

Cramer, R. J. (2004). *Diploma mills: Federal employees have obtained degrees from diploma mills and other unaccredited schools, some at government expense* (GAO-04–771T). Washington, DC: U.S. General Accounting Office.

Davis, M. F. (1994). Challenging the deceptive practices of proprietary schools under the federal false claims act. *Clearinghouse Review, 28*(1), 2–11.

Deil-Amen, R., and Rosenbaum, J. E. (2003, March). The social prerequisites of success: Can college structure reduce the need for social know-how? *Annals of the American Academy of Political and Social Science, 586,* 120–143.

Doherty, G. P. (1973). Case study: The Bell and Howell schools. In D. W. Vermilye (Ed.), *The future in the making* (pp. 182–189). San Francisco: Jossey-Bass.

Dorfman, J. R. (1984, February 27). Instant grades. *Forbes, 133,* 177.

Duff's Business Institute. (2005). *About the college.* Retrieved April 7, 2005, from http://www.duffs-institute.com/.

Dynarski, M. (1994). Who defaults on student loans? Findings from the National Postsecondary Student Aid Study. *Economics of Education Review, 13*(1), 55–68.

Eaton, J. S. (2001, March/April). Regional accreditation reform: Who is served? *Change,* 39–45.

Education Commission of the States. (2000). *Report from the regions: Accreditors' perceptions of the role and impact of for-profit institutions in higher education* (Issue Brief: Accreditation). Denver: Education Commission of the States.

Education Commission of the States. (2005). *Postsecondary governance structures database.* Retrieved April 8, 2005, from http://www.ecs.org/html/educationIssues/Governance/GovPSDB_intro.asp.

Education Management Corporation. (2004). *Brown Mackie college fact sheet.* Pittsburgh: Education Management Corporation.

Erwin, J. M. (1975). *The proprietary school: Assessing its impact on the collegiate sector.* Ann Arbor: Center for the Study of Higher Education, University of Michigan. (ED 145 791)

Federal Trade Commission. (2005a). *Avoid fake-degree burns by researching academic credentials* (FTC Facts for Business). Washington, DC: Bureau of Consumer Protection, Office of Consumer and Business Education.

Federal Trade Commission. (2005b). *Diploma mills: Degrees of deception* (FTC Consumer Alert). Washington, DC: Bureau of Consumer Protection, Office of Consumer and Business Education.

Fitzgerald, B., and Harmon, L. (1988). *Consumer rights and accountability in post-secondary vocational-technical education: An exploratory study.* Washington, DC: Office of Planning, Budget, and Evaluation, U.S. Department of Education. (ED 290 921)

Floyd, C. E. (2005). For-profit degree-granting colleges: Who are these guys and what do they mean for students, traditional institutions, and public policy? In J. C. Smart (Ed.), *Higher education: Handbook of theory and research* (vol. 20, pp. 539–589). Dordrecht, the Netherlands: Springer Publishers.

Forest, J. (2002). *I prefer to teach: An international study of faculty who prefer teaching over research.* New York: RoutledgeFalmer Press.

Frazier, F. (1990). *School accreditation: Activities of seven agencies that accredit proprietary schools* (GAO/HRD-90–179BR). Washington, DC: U.S. General Accounting Office.

Friedlander, M. C. (1980). *Characteristics of students attending proprietary schools and factors influencing their choice* (Monograph 501). Cincinnati: South-Western Publishing Co.

Fulton, R. A. (1969). Proprietary schools. In R. L. Ebel (Ed.), *Encyclopedia of Educational Research* (4th ed., pp. 1022–1027). New York: Macmillan.

Growth cum laude. (1981, September 1). *Financial World,* 43–44.

Grubb, W. N. (1989). *Access, achievement, completion, and "milling around" in postsecondary vocational education.* Berkeley, CA: MPR Associates/National Assessment of Vocational Education.

Grubb, W. N. (1993). The long-run effects of proprietary schools on wages and earnings: Implications for federal policy. *Education Evaluation and Policy Analysis, 15*(1), 17–33.

Grubb, W. N., and Lazerson, M. (2004). *The education gospel: The economic power of schooling.* Cambridge, MA: Harvard University Press.

Gruver, M. (2005, April 6). Online college with no license still open. Associated Press.

Hamilton, W. J. (1958). *The regulation of proprietary schools in the United States.* Unpublished Dissertation, University of Pennsylvania, Philadelphia, PA.

Hayes, B. R., and Jackson, H. P. (1935). *A history of business education in the United States.* Cincinnati: South-Western Publishing Co.

Herrick, C. A. (1904). *Meaning and practice of commercial education.* New York: Macmillan.

Horn, L., and Carroll, C. D. (1996). *Nontraditional undergraduates: Trends in enrollment from 1986 to 1992 and persistence and attainment among 1989–90 beginning postsecondary students* (NCES 97–578). Washington, DC: Office of Educational Research and Improvement, U.S. Department of Education.

Horn, L., Khazzoom, A., and Carroll, C. D. (1993). *Profile of undergraduates in U.S. postsecondary education institutions: 1989–90* (NCES 93–091). Washington, DC: Office of Educational Research and Improvement, U.S. Department of Education.

Hoyt, K. B. (1965). High school guidance and the specialty oriented student research program. *The Vocational Guidance Quarterly, 13*(4), 229–236.

Hyde, W. D. (1976). *Metropolitan vocational proprietary schools: Assessing their role in the U.S. educational systems.* Lexington, MA: Lexington Books.

Internal Revenue Service. (2003). *Publication 557: Tax-exempt status for your organization* (Catalog Number 46573C). Washington, DC: U.S. Department of the Treasury.

International directory of company histories. (1988–2004). Chicago: St. James Press.

James, E. J. (1900). Commercial education. In N. M. Butler (Ed.), *Monographs on education in the United States* (vol. 2, pp. 653–704). Albany, NY: J. B. Lyon Co.

Jeffers, E. (2002). *The History Timeline of the Barbering.* Retrieved December 3, 2004, from http://www.edjeffersbarbermuseum.com/barbertimeline.html.

Jones, J. H. (1973). Proprietary schools as a national resource. In D. W. Vermilye (Ed.), *The future in the making* (pp. 177–181). San Francisco: Jossey-Bass.

Jung, S. M. (1980). *Proprietary vocational education.* Columbus, OH: National Center for Research in Vocational Education. (ED 186 760)

Jung, S. M., Campbell, V. N., and Wolman, J. M. (1976). A comparative study of proprietary and nonproprietary vocational training graduates. *Journal of Vocational Behavior, 8,* 209–225.

Kaplan, W. A. (1971, Summer). The *Marjorie Webster* decisions on accreditation. *Educational Record,* 219–224.

Kaplan, W. A., and Lee, B. A. (1995). *The law of higher education: A comprehensive guide to legal implications of administrative decision making* (3rd ed.). San Francisco: Jossey-Bass.

Kelly, K. F. (2001). *Meeting the needs and making profits: The rise of the for-profit degree-granting institutions.* Denver: Education Commission of the States.

Kerins, F. J. (1989). A case against regional accreditation of single purpose institutions. *NCA Quarterly, 64*(2), 423–426.

Kezar, A. J., Chambers, T. C., and Burkhardt, J. C. (Eds.). (2005). *Higher education for the public good: Emerging voices from a national movement.* San Francisco: Jossey-Bass.

King, R. (2004). The rise and regulation of for-profit higher education. In S. Bjarnason (Ed.), *Mapping borderless higher education: Policy, markets and competition. Selected reports from the Observatory on Borderless Higher Education* (pp. 154–197). London: Observatory on Borderless Higher Education.

Kinser, K. (2002a). GI bill. In J. Forest and K. Kinser (Eds.), *Higher education in the United States: An encyclopedia* (pp. 276–279). Santa Barbara, CA: ABC-Clio.

Kinser, K. (2002b). Taking WGU seriously: Implications of the Western Governors University. *Innovative Higher Education, 26*(3), 161–173.

Kinser, K. (2004a, November 4). *Sources of legitimacy in the private sector: For-profit higher education in the United States.* Paper presented at a meeting of the Association for the Study of Higher Education, Kansas City, MO.

Kinser, K. (2004b, November 4). *What is for-profit higher education?* Paper presented at a meeting of the Association for the Study of Higher Education, Kansas City, MO.

Kinser, K. (2005a). *Accreditation status of U.S. for-profit institutions.* Unpublished data. Albany: University at Albany, State University of New York.

Kinser, K. (2005b). Faculty in for-profit higher education: The University of Phoenix. In D. C. Levy, A. Gupta, and K. B. Powar (Eds.), *Indian and international private higher education.* New Delhi: Deep & Deep.

Kinser, K. (2005c, March 22). *The future of student affairs: Lessons from the for-profit sector.* Paper presented at a meeting of the National Association of Student Affairs Administrators, Tampa, FL.

Kinser, K. (2005d). A profile of regionally accredited for-profit institutions of higher education. In B. Pusser (Ed.), *Arenas of entrepreneurship: Where nonprofit and for-profit institutions compete* (pp. 69–84). San Francisco: Jossey-Bass.

Kinser, K., and Levy, D. C. (2005). For-profit higher education: U.S. tendencies, international echoes. In J. Forest and P. Altbach (Eds.), *The international handbook of higher education.* Dordrecht, the Netherlands, & London: Springer Publishers.

Kirp, D. L. (2003). *Shakespeare, Einstein, and the bottom line: The marketing of higher education.* Cambridge, MA: Harvard University Press.

Knapp, L. G., and others. (2004). *Staff in postsecondary institutions, fall 2002, and salaries of full-time instructional faculty, 2002–03* (NCES 2005–167). Washington, DC: National Center for Education Statistics, U.S. Department of Education.

Knepper, E. G. (1941). *History of business education in United States.* Ann Arbor: Edward Brothers, Inc.

Knight, J. (2004, August 9). Education stocks offer a lesson in unfairness. *Washington Post,* E1.

Koerner, J. D. (1970a, Summer). The case of Marjorie Webster. *Public Interest, 20,* 43–64.

Koerner, J. D. (1970b). *The Parsons College bubble: A tale of higher education in America.* New York: Basic Books.

Krantz, M. (2004, September 21). Remember tracking stocks? Most are history. *USA Today,* 1B.

Kroft, S. (2005, January 30). An expensive lesson, *60 Minutes.* New York: CBS News.

Land, R. H. (1938). Henrico and its college. *William & Mary College Quarterly Historical Magazine, 18*(4), 453–498.

Leatherman, C. (1995, July 14). ABA antitrust settlement spurs questions for other accreditors. *Chronicle of Higher Education,* A15.

Lechuga, V. M. (2003, November 14). *Teachers of the night: Part-time faculty working environments at for-profit institutions.* Paper presented at a meeting of the Association for the Study of Higher Education, Portland, OR.

Lechuga, V. M. (2004, November 4). *New academy/different faculty: Faculty culture at for-profit colleges and universities.* Paper presented at a meting of the Association for the Study of Higher Education, Kansas City, MO.

Lechuga, V. M., Tierney, W. G., and Hentschke, G. C. (2003). *Expanding the horizon: For-profit degree granting institutions of higher education: An annotated bibliography.* Los Angeles: Center for Higher Education Policy Analysis, Rossier School of Education, University of Southern California.

Lee, J. B. (1990). Who defaults on student loans? *Career Training, 6*(3), 30–33.

Lee, J. B., and Merisotis, J. P. (1990). *Proprietary schools: Programs, policies, and prospects.* ASHE-ERIC Higher Education Report no. 5. Washington, DC: School of Education and Human Development, The George Washington University.

Lipinsky de Orlov, L. S., Jr. (1981). *Katharine Gibbs School (Inc.) v. FTC:* Restricting the Federal Trade Commission's trade regulation rulemaking authority under the Magnuson-Moss Act. *New York University Law Review, 56*(1), 183–205.

Marchese, T. (1998, May/June). Not-so-distant competitors: How new providers are remaking the postsecondary marketplace. *AAHE Bulletin,* 3–11.

Mendes, J. (1988, November 21). A play on educating America's workforce. *Forbes, 118,* 50–52.

Merisotis, J. P., and Shedd, J. M. (2003). Using IPEDS to develop a classification system for two-year postsecondary institutions. In A. C. McCormick and R. D. Cox (Eds.), *Classification systems for two-year colleges* (pp. 47–62). San Francisco: Jossey-Bass.

Merwin, J. (1981, October 26). Have lectures, will travel. *Forbes, 128,* 87–90.

Miller, J. W., and Hamilton, W. J. (1964). *The independent business school in American education.* New York: McGraw-Hill.

Moore, R. W. (1995). The illusion of convergence: Federal student aid policy in community colleges and proprietary schools. In D. A. Clowes and E. M. Hawthorne (Eds.), *Community colleges and proprietary schools: Conflict or convergence?* (pp. 71–80). San Francisco: Jossey-Bass.

Morey, A. (2004). Globalization and the emergence of for-profit higher education. *Higher Education, 48*(1), 131–152.

National Center for Education Statistics. (1991). *Digest of education statistics* (NCES 91–660). Washington, DC: U.S. Department of Education.

National Center for Education Statistics. (2000). *Digest of education statistics, 1999* (NCES 2000–031). Washington, DC: U.S. Department of Education.

National Center for Education Statistics. (2002). *Classification of instructional programs* (NCES 2002-165). Washington, DC: U.S. Department of Education.

National Center for Education Statistics. (2003a). *Digest of education statistics, 2002* (NCES 2003–060). Washington, DC: U.S. Department of Education.

National Center for Education Statistics. (2003b). *Postsecondary institutions in the United States: Fall 2002 and degrees and other awards conferred: 2001–02* (NCES 2004–154). Washington, DC: U.S. Department of Education.

National Center for Education Statistics. (2004a). *College opportunities online.* Retrieved October 29, 2004, from http://nces.ed.gov/ipeds/cool.

National Center for Education Statistics. (2004b). *Digest of education statistics, 2003* (NCES 2005–025). Washington, DC: U.S. Department of Education.

National Center for Education Statistics. (2005). *Enrollment in postsecondary institutions: Fall 2002 and financial statistics, fiscal year 2002* (NCES 2005–168). Washington, DC: U.S. Department of Education.

National education: A leader in a new growth industry. (1980, November). *Dun's Review,* 132–133.

Newman, F., Couturier, L., and Scurry, J. (2004). *The future of higher education: Rhetoric, reality, and the risks of the market.* San Francisco: Jossey-Bass.

Noble, D. F. (1997). *Digital diploma mills.* Retrieved January 6, 2005, from http://www.firstmonday.dk/issues/issue3_1/noble/.

Office of Degree Authorization. (2005). *Diploma mills.* Retrieved March 10, 2005, from http://www.osac.state.or.us/oda.

Ortmann, A. (2001). Capital romance: Why Wall Street fell in love with higher education. *Education Economics, 9*(3), 293–311.

Pascarella, E. T., and Terenzini, P. T. (2005). *How college affects students: A third decade of research.* San Francisco: Jossey-Bass.

Persell, C. H., and Wenglinsky, H. (2004). For-profit postsecondary education and civic engagement. *Higher Education, 47,* 337–359.

Petrello, G. J. (1987). *In service to America: AICS at 75.* New York: McGraw-Hill.

Phillips, S. (2004, November 26). Selling out to get "asses in classes." *Times Higher Education Supplement,* 19.

Phipps, R. A., Harrison, K. V., and Merisotis, J. P. (1999). *Students at private, for-profit institutions* (NCES 2000–175). Washington, DC: National Center For Education Statistics, U.S. Department of Education.

Pusser, B., and Doane, D. J. (2001, September/October). Public purposes and private enterprise: The contemporary organization of postsecondary education. *Change,* 19–22.

Pusser, B., and Wolcott, D. A. (2003, November 14). *A crowded lobby: Nonprofit and for-profit universities in the emerging politics of higher education.* Paper presented at a meeting of the Association for the Study of Higher Education, Portland, OR.

Reigner, C. G. (1959). *Beginnings of the business school.* Baltimore: H. M. Rowe Co.

Rhode Island Board of Governors for Higher Education. (2004). *Regulations governing institutions of higher education operating in Rhode Island.* Providence: Rhode Island Office of Higher Education.

Roey, S., Skinner, R. R., Fernandez, R., and Barbett, S. (1999). *Fall staff in postsecondary institutions, 1997* (NCES 2000–164). Washington, DC: National Center for Education Statistics, U.S. Department of Education.

Ruch, R. S. (2001). *Higher ed, inc.: The rise of the for-profit university.* Baltimore: Johns Hopkins University Press.

Sachdev, A. (2004, July 18). School's stocks get bad grades. *Chicago Tribune.*

St. John, E. P., Starkey, J. B., Paulson, M. B., and Mbaduagha, L. A. (1995). The influence of prices and price subsidies on within year persistence by students in proprietary schools. *Educational Evaluation and Policy Studies, 17*(2), 149–165.

Salinas, M. A., and Monagle, L. L. (1991). *Proprietary vocational schools: Selected references, 1965–1991* (91–312 L). Washington, DC: Congressional Research Service.

Schenet, M. A. (1990). *Proprietary schools: The regulatory structure* (90–424 EPW). Washington, DC: Congressional Research Service.

Seybolt, R. F. (1971). *Source studies in American colonial education: The private school.* New York: Arno Press.

Shareholder suit hits Apollo. (2004, October 19). *Arizona Republic.*

Shoemaker, E. A. (1973, Summer). Community colleges: The challenge of proprietary schools. *Change,* 71–72.

Slaughter, S., and Rhoades, G. (2004). *Academic capitalism in the new economy.* Baltimore: Johns Hopkins University Press.

Smith, N. B. (1999). A tribute to the visionaries, prime movers and pioneers of vocational education, 1892 to 1917. *Journal of Vocational and Technical Education, 16*(1). Available: http://scholar.lib.vt.edu/ejournals/JVTE/v16n1/smith.html. Accessed: November 9, 2005.

Snyder, T. D. (Ed.). (1993). *120 years of American education: A statistical portrait.* Washington, DC: Office of Educational Research and Improvement, U.S. Department of Education.

Sperling, J. (2000). *Rebel with a cause: The entrepreneur who created the University of Phoenix and the for-profit revolution in higher education.* New York: Wiley.

Sperling, J., and Tucker, R. W. (1997). *For-profit higher education: Developing a world-class workforce.* New Brunswick, NJ: Transaction.

Stein, D. (Ed.). (2004). *Buying in or selling out? The commercialization of the American research university.* Piscataway, NJ: Rutgers University Press.

Strosnider, K. (1998, January 23). Higher education for profit. *Chronicle of Higher Education,* A36.

Thompson, R. (1989). A case for regional accreditation of single purpose institutions. *NCA Quarterly, 64*(2), 417–422.

Trivett, D. A. (1974). *Proprietary schools and postsecondary education.* ERIC Higher Education Research Report No. 2. Washington, DC: American Association for Higher Education.

Twigg, C. A. (1996). Is technology a silver bullet? *Educom Review, 31*(2). Available: http://www.educause.edu/apps/er/review/reviewArticles/31228.html. Accessed November 9, 2005.

U.S. Department of Education. (1973). Higher education general information survey (HEGIS), 1972–1973: Institutional characteristics [Computer file]. ICPSR version. Washington, DC: National Center for Education Statistics, U.S. Dept. of Education.

U.S. Department of Education. (1999). The secretary's recognition of accrediting agencies, 34 CFR Part 602. *Federal Register, 64*(202), 56612–56626.

U.S. Department of Education. (2004). *Accreditation in the United States.* Retrieved October 21, 2004, from http://www.ed.gov/admins/finaid/accred/.

U.S. Department of Education. (2005). *Distance education demonstration program: Program participants.* Retrieved February 15, 2005, from http://www.ed.gov/programs/disted/participants.html.

U.S. Department of Justice. (1995, June 27). Justice department and American Bar Association resolve charges that the ABA's process for accrediting law schools was misused. Press Release. Washington, DC: U.S. Department of Justice.

U.S. Office of Education. (1942). *Biennial survey of education, 1940–42* (vol. 2). Washington, DC: U.S. Government Printing Office.

Van Dyne, L. (1974, December 16). Accreditors drop ban on proprietaries. *Chronicle of Higher Education,* 6.

Venn, G. (1964). *Man, education and work: Postsecondary vocational and technical education.* Washington, DC: American Council on Education.

Veysey, L. R. (1965). *The emergence of the American university.* Chicago: University of Chicago Press.

Walden University. (2003). *2003–2004 catalog.* Minneapolis: Walden University.

Wei, C. C., Li, X., and Berkner, L. (2004). *A decade of undergraduate student aid: 1989–90 to 1999–2000* (NCES 2004–158). Washington DC: National Center for Education Statistics, U.S. Department of Education.

Whitehead, J. S. (1973). *The separation of college and state: Columbia, Dartmouth, Harvard, and Yale, 1776–1876.* New Haven, CT: Yale University Press.

Williams, G., and Woodhall, M. (1979). *Independent further education.* London: Policy Studies Institute.

Wilms, W. W. (1974). *Public and proprietary vocational training: A study of effectiveness.* Berkeley, CA: Center for Research and Development in Higher Education, University of California, Berkeley.

Wilms, W. W. (1983). Proprietary schools and student financial aid. *Journal of Financial Aid, 13*(2), 7–17.

Wilms, W. W. (1987, January/February). Proprietary schools: Strangers in their own land. *Change,* 10–22.

Wilms, W. W., and Hansell, S. (1983, Spring). The dubious promise of postsecondary vocational education: Its payoff to dropouts and graduates in the U.S.A. *International Journal of Educational Development, 2,* 43–59.

Winston, G. C. (1999). For-profit higher education: Godzilla or Chicken Little? *Change, 31*(1), 12–19.

Wright, B. (1988). For the children of the infidels? American Indian education in the colonial colleges. *American Indian Culture and Research Journal, 12*(3), 1–14.

Young, K. E. (1987, March). Accrediting organizations: You can't tell the players without a program. *Career Training,* 8–10.

Name Index

A

Adelman, C., 4, 75
Allen, I. E., 5
Alstete, J. W., 100, 106
Altbach, P. G., 95
Apling, R. N., 4, 70, 73, 82, 134

B

Badway, N., 3, 29, 76, 78, 81, 84, 88
Bailey, T. R., 3, 29, 30, 31, 59, 60, 76, 7, 81, 84, 88
Barbett, S., 90
Barker, A., 109
Bartlett, R. M., 16
Bartlett, T., 87
Becker, D., 58
Belitsky, A. H., 9, 22, 26, 27, 68, 69, 86, 89, 94
Bennett, J. G., 15q
Berg, G. A., 23, 86, 134
Berkner, L., 118
Blumenstyk, G., 24, 88
Bok, D., 1, 9
Bolino, A. C., 9, 16, 66, 67, 89, 100
Bollag, B., 87
Breneman, D., 29, 86, 92, 93, 94, 126, 127, 130, 134
Brimah, T., 114
Bryant, H. B., 18

Burd, S., 24
Burgan, M., 109
Burkhardt, J. C., 130
Byce, C., 73

C

Campbell, V. N., 4, 69, 74
Carroll, C. D., 71, 72
Chaloux, B. N., 21, 113, 114, 115
Chambers, T. C., 130
Cheng, X. D., 70
Chung, A., 74
Clark, H. F., 5, 9, 82
Collins, S., 121, 122, 123
Coughlin, E., 105
Couturier, L., 1
Cramer, R. J., 121, 122

D

Davis, M. F., 4, 120
Deil-Amen, R., 78
DeVry, H., 51
Doane, D. J., 23
Doherty, G. P., 22, 41
Donoho, T., 59
Dorfman, J. R., 43
Dynarski, M., 4, 71

Wilms, W., 4, 41, 43, 69, 72, 73, 74, 86
Winston, G. C., 5, 23, 29
Wolcott, D. A., 61
Wolman, J. M., 4, 69, 74

Woodhall, M., 41
Wright, B., 13

Y

Young, K. E., 107

Subject Index

A

Academic models, 85–87, 128
Academic outcomes for students, 74–77, 94–96
Accreditation
  background on, 98–99
  financial aid and, 20–22, 37, 97, 99, 100–102, 123
  history of, 100–102
  regional, 32, 102–106
  shopping, 108–110
Accrediting agencies, 26, 27, 106–108
Admission requirements, 87–89
Apollo Group, 22, 23, 40, 45, 46–47, 49, 58, 91, 119, 134

B

Business college era, 17–19
Business curriculum, 81–83

C

Career connector institutions, 28
Career Education Corporation (CEC), 6, 40, 48–49, 91, 118
Certificate institutions, 28, 76, 84, 85
Civic responsibility in students, 76–77
Classification of institutions
  difficulties with, 35–38

early attempts at, 25–27
ECS model for, 28–30
new, 30–35
Concorde Career Colleges, 40, 45, 49–50
Corinthian Colleges, 30, 40, 44, 45, 50–51, 63, 91, 119, 134
Corporate ownership, impact of, viii, 5, 22–24, 61–63. *See also* Shareholder institutions
Curriculum
  academic models, 85–87, 128
  admissions requirements, 87–89
  business, 81–83
  degrees, 5, 32, 76, 83–85, 126

D

Degrees
  corporate expansion and, 5
  description of, 83–85
  highest degree awarded, 31, 32
  percentage awarded, 76, 85, 126
DeVry
  description of, 51–52
  faculty, 91, 94
  general education at, 95
  as huge chain, 25
  as shareholder institution, 5, 33, 35, 39, 40, 41, 44, 45
  student satisfaction at, 77–78
Diploma mills, 6, 120–122

Distance education
corporate expansion and, 5
Internet institutions, 28, 29
in public colleges and universities,
122–123
Title IV financial aid and, 134.
See also University of Phoenix
Diversity, institutional, 25–38

E
Education Commission of the States
(ECS), 28–30, 107, 108, 113, 114, 115
Education Management Corporation
(EDMC), 33, 40, 52–53, 63, 91
85-15 rule, 117, 124
Enterprise institutions, 28, 29, 30, 32, 34
Eras of for-profit higher education, 14,
16–23
EVCI Career Colleges, 23, 40, 45, 54–55

F
Faculty
description of, 89–90
full-time, 90–91
role of, 87, 92–94
student-faculty ratio, 92
False Claims Act, 120
Federal oversight, 111, 115–120, 121
Federal student aid era, 14, 20–22, 97,
123–124
Federal Trade Commission (FTC), ix, 6,
112, 116–117, 118, 120, 121, 122, 123
Financial aid, federal
accreditation and, 37, 97, 99, 100–102,
123
era of, 14, 20–22, 97
regulatory issues and, 123–124
For-profit higher education
conclusions on, 130–131
defined, 7–10
historical perspective on, 6, 13–24
lack of information on, 2–4
new prominence of, 1–11

For-profit institutions
accreditation of, 97–110
classifications of, 25–38
curriculum at, 81–89
faculty at, 89–94
intellectual development and, 94–96
regulation of, 111–124
students at, 65–79
tax codes and, 7
types of, 33–35

G
Gender differences in enrollment, xiii,
66–67, 73
GI bill, 20, 21, 66, 67, 100, 113,
115–116, 125

H
Higher Education Act (HEA), ix, 6, 8, 9,
10, 20–21, 68, 100, 102, 111, 113, 116,
122, 123–124, 134, 135
Highest degree awarded, 31, 32
History of for-profit education, 6, 13–24,
100–102, 129
History of shareholder institutions, 39,
41–45

I
Institutional accreditation, defined,
98–99
International expansion, research on, 129
Internet institutions, 28, 29, 30. *See also*
University of Phoenix
ITT Educational Services, 40, 55–56,
91, 119
ITT Technical Institute, 25, 42, 55

K
Kaplan Higher Education, 40, 46, 56–57
KinderCare Learning Centers, 57

University of Phoenix (UOP)
accreditation of, 103–104,
108, 109
as dominant institution, 5, 6
education majors at, 83
enrollment data, 25, 36–37, 126
faculty at, 91, 93
online campuses, 126, 135
regulatory issues and, 119, 122
as shareholder institution, 33, 35,
46–47
student recruitment at, 89
Wall Street era and, 22, 23

V

Venture institutions, 32, 34

W

Wall Street era
academic mission during, 81
defined, 14, 22–24
implications of, 61–63, 127, 130–131
Westwood College, 30
Women
faculty, 89
students, viii, 66–67, 71, 73

About the Author

Kevin Kinser is an assistant professor in the Department of Educational Administration and Policy Studies at the State University of New York at Albany. He received two master's degrees and a doctorate from Columbia University's Teachers College and has taught in the higher education programs at Teachers College and Louisiana State University. Before his doctoral studies, Kinser worked in student affairs at Beloit College and Columbia University, serving as an administrator of student activities and student union operations. As a researcher, Kinser studies nontraditional and alternative higher education, particularly the organization and administration of for-profit and virtual universities. He also is interested in the various ways in which institutions of higher education choose to serve and support students. He is the coeditor, with James JF Forest, of *Higher Education in the United States: An Encyclopedia* (ABC-CLIO, 2002), a comprehensive two-volume overview of American postsecondary education since World War II.

About the ASHE Higher Education Reports Series

Since 1983, the ASHE (formerly ASHE-ERIC) Higher Education Report Series has been providing researchers, scholars, and practitioners with timely and substantive information on the critical issues facing higher education. Each monograph presents a definitive analysis of a higher education problem or issue, based on a thorough synthesis of significant literature and institutional experiences. Topics range from planning to diversity and multiculturalism, to performance indicators, to curricular innovations. The mission of the Series is to link the best of higher education research and practice to inform decision making and policy. The reports connect conventional wisdom with research and are designed to help busy individuals keep up with the higher education literature. Authors are scholars and practitioners in the academic community. Each report includes an executive summary, review of the pertinent literature, descriptions of effective educational practices, and a summary of key issues to keep in mind to improve educational policies and practice.

The Series is one of the most peer reviewed in higher education. A National Advisory Board made up of ASHE members reviews proposals. A National Review Board of ASHE scholars and practitioners reviews completed manuscripts. Six monographs are published each year and they are approximately 120 pages in length. The reports are widely disseminated through Jossey-Bass and John Wiley & Sons, and they are available online to subscribing institutions through Wiley InterScience (http://www.interscience.wiley.com).

Call for Proposals

The ASHE Higher Education Report Series is actively looking for proposals. We encourage you to contact one of the editors, Dr. Kelly Ward (kaward@wsu.edu) or Dr. Lisa Wolf-Wendel (lwolf@ku.edu), with your ideas.

Recent Titles

Back Issue/Subscription Order Form

Copy or detach and send to:
Jossey-Bass, A Wiley Imprint, 989 Market Street, San Francisco CA 94103-1741

Call or fax toll-free: Phone 888-378-2537 6:30AM – 3PM PST; Fax 888-481-2665

Back Issues: Please send me the following issues at $26 each
(Important: please include series abbreviation and issue number.
For example AEHE 28:1)

_____

_____

_____

$ _____   Total for single issues

$ _____   SHIPPING CHARGES: SURFACE   Domestic Canadian
                                    First Item $5.00 $6.00
                                    Each Add'l Item $3.00 $1.50
                 For next-day and second-day delivery rates, call the number listed above.

Subscriptions   Please ❑ start ❑ renew my subscription to *ASHE Higher Education
                 Reports* for the year 2_____ at the following rate:

                 U.S.   ❑ Individual $165   ❑ Institutional $185
                 Canada   ❑ Individual $165   ❑ Institutional $245
                 All Others   ❑ Individual $201   ❑ Institutional $296
                 ❑ Online subscriptions available too!

                 **For more information about online subscriptions, visit
                 www.interscience.wiley.com**

$ _____   Total single issues and subscriptions (Add appropriate sales tax
                 for your state for single issue orders. No sales tax for U.S.
                 subscriptions. Canadian residents, add GST for subscriptions and
                 single issues.)

❑Payment enclosed (U.S. check or money order only)
❑VISA ❑ MC ❑ AmEx ❑ #_____ Exp. Date _____

Signature _____ Day Phone _____
❑ Bill Me (U.S. institutional orders only. Purchase order required.)

Purchase order # _____
                 Federal Tax ID13559302   GST 89102 8052

Name _____

Address _____

_____

Phone _____ E-mail _____

For more information about Jossey-Bass, visit our Web site at www.josseybass.com